I0041279

Zend Framework 1 to 2 Migration Guide

by

Bart McLeod

▲ a php[architect] guide

Zend Framework 1 to 2 Migration Guide

Contents Copyright ©2015 Bart McLeod—All Rights Reserved

Book and cover layout, design and text Copyright ©2015 musketeers.me, LLC. and its predecessors—All Rights Reserved. Print and Digital copies available from _https://www.phparch.com/books/_

First Edition: October 2015
ISBN - Print: **978-1-940111-21-6**
ISBN - PDF: **978-1-940111-22-3**
ISBN - ePub: **978-1-940111-23-0**
ISBN - Mobi: **978-1-940111-24-7**
ISBN - Safari: **978-1-940111-25-4**
Produced & Printed in the United States

No part of this book may be reproduced, stored in a public retrieval system, or publicly transmitted in any form or by means without the prior written permission of the publisher, except in the case of brief quotations embedded in critical reviews or articles.

Disclaimer

Although every effort has been made in the preparation of this book to ensure the accuracy of the information contained therein, this book is provided "as-is" and the publisher, the author(s), their distributors and retailers, as well as all affiliated, related or subsidiary parties take no responsibility for any inaccuracy and any and all damages caused, either directly or indirectly, by the use of such information. We have endeavored to properly provide trademark information on all companies and products mentioned in the book by the appropriate use of capitals. However, we cannot guarantee the accuracy of such information.

musketeers.me, the musketeers.me logo, php[architect], the php[architect] logo, NanoBook and the NanoBook logo are trademarks or registered trademarks of musketeers.me, LLC, its assigns, partners, predecessors and successors.

Written by
Bart McLeod

Published by
musketeers.me, LLC.
201 Adams Ave.
Alexandria, VA 22301
USA

240-348-5PHP (240-348-5747)

info@phparch.com
www.phparch.com

Editor-in-Chief
Oscar Merida

Managing Editor
Eli White

Technical Reviewer
Matthew Setter

Layout and Design
Kevin Bruce

Table of Contents

Preface

Introduction

Zend Framework (ZF) 2, the successor to Zend Framework 1, saw its first stable release in September 2012. By the time I'll have finished this guide, ZF2 will have been available for much longer. There are two main reasons that you might have opened this guide for reading.

The first is that you're already a Zend Framework developer and didn't get the chance to follow the development of ZF2. Now you want to catch up quickly by comparing ZF1 to ZF2. The second is somewhat different; you are faced with the challenge of migrating a ZF1 MVC application to ZF2. In that case, you must understand that ZF2 is not just an upgrade compared to ZF1; it is mostly a new product.

Practical Guide

Although I might try to explain the abstract concepts behind some of the new features of ZF2, in terms of design patterns, there are others who are better at academic explanations. My goal is to provide you with an easy-to-use guide that addresses common issues you are likely to encounter. For example: if you used a certain view helper in ZF1, what would it look like in ZF2, and how will you actually make your ZF2 application aware of the existence of it?

Chapter 1

Quick start: Zend_Tool versus ZendSkeletonApplication

Zend_Tool could be used in ZF1 to generate a *new* ZF project for you and to add controllers and other stuff to *existing* ZF projects. If you never knew you used Zend_Tool, that's no problem at all. If you used ZendStudio to create new ZF projects, it was using Zend_Tool under the hood. It's also possible that you built your project from scratch, all by yourself, or that you simply inherited a code base.

ZF2 offers a small, basic application that only presents one static page, one that you can change in order to build your own application. Changing it would mean adding modules and configuration options. It's called ZendSkeletonApplication, and it's available from GitHub or as a downloadable archive at *https://github.com/zendframework/ZendSkeletonApplication*.

There is also a separate project called ZFTool, which can install a
ZendSkeletonApplication for you. It can also do other things, such as
adding a module. This is under active development, and you can find it at
https://github.com/zendframework/ZFTool.

In addition, if you want to use ZFTool, it is best installed using Composer. Composer is
a dependency manager that you can use to install php libraries and applications. If you
are familiar with Composer, this will be great news for you. If not, Composer might
present another hurdle to overcome, and you'd better skip it until you're ready for it. If
you are unfamiliar with Composer and want to start making convenient installations
from the command line right from the beginning, then please read the chapter on
Development Practices.

The Migration Process

For a migration project, I strongly recommend that you use the
ZendSkeletonApplication, moving elements into it from your existing ZF1
application one by one, starting with the easiest parts. This allows you to gradually learn
the concepts of ZF2, leveraging them when you get to the harder parts.

Example Projects

This guide comes with two projects, which you can download from GitHub and are
equivalent in terms of functionality. One is built on ZF1, and the other is built on ZF2. The
functionality by itself is trivial, as it only demonstrates the differences between the two
versions of the framework. The ZF1 example has been set up using Zend_Tool, while the
ZF2 example is a clone of the ZendSkeletonApplication with an extra module, called
Book, which contains the examples. You will learn about modules in ZF2 later on.

Zend_Tool is used as follows:

```
zf create project book
```

The versions I used were the latest versions from version control (svn for ZF1 and Git for
ZF2). When I started the projects, these versions were ZF1.12.0 and ZF2.0.4. At publication,
ZF2 was at 2.4.1.

For both projects, the ZF library had to be in a certain directory inside the project.
For ZF1, it has to be library/Zend by default. In ZF2, the default location is
vendor/ZF2/library/Zend. If you only download the ZendSkeletonApplication
and then run a composer installation from inside it, it will download and install the ZF2
library for you. But you can also download it yourself and just place it in vendor such
that the libraries are in the path mentioned above.

Chapter 2

Zend Framework 2 Overview

For this migration guide, I will assume that you are using ZF1 as an MVC application (*more about MVC in the next chapter*) and that you also intend to use ZF2 that way.

Less Magic

The way MVC has implemented changes in ZF2, there is less *magic* going on. Many things that happened magically in ZF1 are carried out explicitly in ZF2. An example of this is how your application loads its view helpers. In ZF1, if you put them in the `helpers` directory, under your `views` directory, the application would auto-magically find them. In ZF2, you have to tell the application how to create your view helpers by configuring each one explicitly. In short, magic has been replaced by configuration.

Modular

ZF2 is built around the concept of reusable modules, which form the foundation of your application. Again, there is no magic when it comes to loading modules. In `config/application.config.php`, you configure which modules are loaded and in which order. The configurations of these modules are *merged* in that same order, but they can be overridden globally if necessary. *This is important to remember!*

The recommended way to write configurations is with PHP arrays because they are both easy to create and the most performant. Additionally, building PHP arrays is something we all master, so no new skills are required to configure your application. However, some knowledge is required so you know *what* to configure and *when*.

Services and Events

As modules are the building blocks of the application, so services are the building blocks of modules. Events wire modules together, making ZF2 fully event-driven. However, this guide is about migration, and ZF1 was not event driven. Consequently, diving into events really deeply is beyond the scope of this book, but we'll cover the common uses of events.

Arrays and Your Code Editor

The configuration arrays of ZF2 are the big stumbling block for developers new to it. While they offer invaluable flexibility and become more readable as you get used to them, they look intimidating at first glance. It's even more intimidating to edit them if your code editor doesn't do the indentation automatically.

Code formatting tools and extensions are available for major IDEs and editors. If your using one that can't be configured to automatically indent arrays the way you can best read them, then I would recommend giving PHPStorm a try. PHPStorm is a really fast and an incredibly smart IDE that does an excellent job of formatting your configuration arrays. You can download the latest version here: *https://www.jetbrains.com/phpstorm*.

> *IDE and editor choices are highly personal, and there are many others—both commercial and Open-source—available. If PHPStorm doesn't suit you, there are many you can try just a web search away. Some other popular IDEs and editors include Eclipse, Netbeans, and SublimeText.*

Classmaps

One of the key performance improvements in ZF2 was the introduction of classmap autoloading. You might encounter them in an existing ZF1 project, as well, as they were back-ported to ZF1. There are other autoloaders available, some of which look more like what we we're used to. But classmap autoloading is easy to use and very fast.

A classmap is no more than an associative array telling PHP which class is in which file. That is, it maps classnames to file system paths. There is a classmap_generator.php script available in the ZF2 source, which will create a classmap for you if you need one for a library, for example.

If you are introducing or converting classes one by one, it is just as easy to type up your classmap as you go; furthermore, each library or namespace can have its own classmap. This is an example of a classmap taken from my pet project 'CuddleFish':

```
$path = __DIR__ . '/CuddleFish/';

return array(
    'CuddleFish\DataObject' => $path . 'DataObject.php',
    'CuddleFish\ListProvider' => $path . 'ListProvider.php',
    'CuddleFish\Globals' => $path . 'Globals.php',
    'CuddleFish\Access' => $path . 'Access.php',
    'CuddleFish\DAGO' => $path . 'DAGO.php',
    'CuddleFish\AdminModule' => $path . 'AdminModule.php',
    'CuddleFish\Auth\Adapter' => $path . 'Auth/Adapter.php',
);
```

Autoloader Configuration

The Module class, which is the only requirement for a module, has a method called getAutoloaderConfig, which returns an array of all of the autoloaders for the module. If you configure a classmap autoloader, you can configure that with a classmap for each namespace or library that you wish to load.

```
public function getAutoloaderConfig()
{
    return array(
        'Zend\Loader\ClassMapAutoloader' => array(
            'Book' => __DIR__ . '/class_map.php',
        ),
    );
}
```

The above example will load all the classes in the Book module or namespace from the classmap in module/Book/class_map.php.

Standard Autoloader

While you are actively developing your module, it is easier to use the standard autoloader, instead of a classmap. This way, you do not have to keep your classmap up-to-date while you keep adding classes:

```
public function getAutoloaderConfig()
{
  return array(
    'Zend\Loader\StandardAutoloader' => array(
      'namespaces' => array(
        __NAMESPACE__ => __DIR__ . '/src/' . __NAMESPACE__,
      ),
    ),
  );
}
```

Note that the configuration array for the standard autoloader has an extra nesting level. This configuration tells the standard autoloader to look for the classes from the Book namespace inside the path module/Book/src/Book. Adding the extra src directory is a convention; it is up to you where you put your classes.

Name Changes

Many names have changed for various reasons. One very important reason is that naming of various components has to be consistent across the framework. Another is that with the introduction of namespaces, which involves changing names by nature, some names are no longer available.

To give an example, you can't replace Zend_View_Helper_Abstract with Zend\View\Helper\Abstract because abstract is a reserved word in PHP. It is simply not possible to execute the following:

```
namespace Zend\View\Helper;

abstract class Abstract {
    //[...]
}
```

Instead, it has become the following: Zend\View\Helper\AbstractHelper.

Zend_Registry is Gone

Zend_Registry was the next big thing after the dreaded Globals class. It was a clever way to get dependencies from a central repository, but it was limited. Once you are calling Zend_Registry::get('log') in two hundred different places and want to use a different log in, say, twenty of those, what are you going to do? What if you want to do that conditionally? What if third-party code also wants to use the log key in the same registry?

ZF2 gets rid of the registry and replaces that with a central object for registering services: the ServiceManager. Objects in need of the ServiceManager can implement the ServiceLocatorAwareInterface, which exposes the getServiceLocator() method. This yields the ServiceManager, which can then be easily asked for all configured dependencies the object might use with the get method of the ServiceManager.

Keys configured with the ServiceManager should follow convention to avoid name clashes, making it easy to change them later, should a name clash occur. You can even configure which keys you use as aliases. An example of a key used to configure a logging service is Book\log.

How do you get your log instance or any other dependency inside your controller if you can't use the registry or something else that is globally available? The answer is to use a factory class or closure, which instantiates your controller.

You will learn more about factories later on. The essence is that the factory has access to the ServiceManager and therefore has access to every service that the manager has been configured with. It can then inject it into your controller before returning it.

jQuery Integration is History

jQuery integration, which was provided by ZendX in ZF1, is now absent and unlikely to return. Given that, you will have to integrate jQuery the normal way. This is just a matter of creating regular <script> tags in the <head> section of the layout template or by using the headScript() view helper, which point to the jQuery source files and a <link> tag for the jQuery stylesheet or use the headLink() view helper for that.

Chapter 3

Model View Controller

Here we go, our first design pattern. Zend Framework offers a Model View Controller (MVC) implementation, but it is also possible to use ZF without using its MVC infrastructure. MVC is about separating *Views* (V) from business logic that is encapsulated in *Models* (M) and the interaction between the two via (C—*Controllers*). The goal is to provide components that are more reusable and easier to test.

ZF, unlike other frameworks at the time, did not tightly couple to the M in MVC. In the ZF philosophy, you, the developer, are the only one who can decide what your business model is about and hence what it's going to look like. ZF developers do not want to make assumptions about that, and because of that, they offer no model implementation out of the box, though there are components you can use. ZF1 and ZF2 both offer views and controllers and an infrastructure to tie those together. While views and controllers have many similarities between both versions of the framework, the wiring is totally different.

Modules

In ZF1, you could have modules, but their behavior wasn't truly modular. A module in ZF1 could not live in another ZF1 application without changing that application or changing the module. The MVC application and the module always ended up sharing things, such as configurations, that they should have used independently. It was almost impossible to pick up a module and drop it into another ZF1 application.

With ZF2, this has changed completely. ZF2 is built entirely around the concept of independent, or drop-in, modules. In fact, even the ZF2 library itself is a module. This doesn't mean that modules can never depend on other modules, nor that they can never have any dependencies, in general. But they should be able to operate inside another application if you move them there, as long as their dependencies are satisfied. Generally speaking, they should not depend on the ZF2 application they are dropped into. In line with this philosophy, if you are going to write a ZF2 application, you are going to write modules.

A good example is ZfcUser (more about that later). ZfcUser depends on ZfcBase (and ZF2). Both ZfcUser and ZfcBase are modules. If you drop both into a ZF2 application and set up and configure the database table for ZfcUser, then you can authenticate users. Nothing else is needed. If you install ZfcUser with Composer, it will install ZfcBase for you because it is configured as a dependency of ZfcUser. Nice and simple.

Dependency Injection

To add the flexibility regarding dependencies that is needed to implement such a truly modular approach, a developer-friendly flavor of the famous Dependency Injection (DI) pattern has been implemented, called Service Locator. The name says it all; if you need something, ask for it. It's like room service for software.

To gain a deeper understanding of the how the ServiceManager works in the context of MVC, you should really read the online documentation for the ServiceManager [1]. It provides a good explanation, but you will need to try it out for yourself to fully appreciate its power.

In ZF2, you write services, which you wire together using events. All the basic wiring is already done for you by the MVC infrastructure, but if you need something fancy, you can either hook into the existing wiring or throw some of your own custom events into the mix.

The events are controlled by an EventManager, and services are managed by a ServiceManager. The ServiceManager *implements* the ServiceLocatorInterface, which means you can pull services out of it by calling its get($key) method with the key that the service was registered with.

[1]   http://framework.zend.com/manual/2.1/en/modules/zend.service-manager.quick-start.html

Event Driven

ZF1 knew of some events. You could, for example, implement a preDispatch method inside your controller or controller plugin, which would be called by the MVC infrastructure at the "right" time. This was more like a hook system, such as those that WordPress and Drupal use. You had little control over what the right time actually was, and you were limited to events that were provided as predefined function names (hooks) that you could either implement or omit.

While you can still implement similar hooks at certain points, ZF2 is fully event driven. You can tie anything to anything else using events, and it will probably take you some time to get used to this and to leverage it to its full potential. ZF2 uses the EventManager for this, and that component is back-ported to ZF1 version 1.12 so that you can now use some of its power in ZF1.

Event Hook Example

Let's compare a controller's preDispatch event hook in ZF1 to its counterpart in ZF2. The code in the event implementation also demonstrates how some names have changed.

Zend Framework 1

```
// inside IndexController
public function preDispatch()
{
    $session = new Zend_Session_Namespace('Fronted');
    $session->hello = 'The session says hello!';
}
```

This is nothing spectacular, but how would you do this in ZF2? You would rename the preDispatch hook to a dispatch hook, and you need to add $request and $response arguments to comply with the hook method signature. It now works if you extended your controller from AbstractActionController, which takes care of the basics for you.

Zend Framework 2

```
// inside IndexController
use Zend\Stdlib\RequestInterface;
use Zend\Stdlib\ResponseInterface;
use Zend\Session\Container as SessionContainer;

public function dispatch(
    RequestInterface $request,
    ResponseInterface $response = null
)
{
    $session = new SessionContainer('Frontend_2');
    $session->hello = 'The session says hello 2!';
    return parent::dispatch($request, $response);
}
```

So by extending the AbstractActionController, you get some basic event hooks for free. The postDispatch hook is gone, but you can use the render hook, which also existed in ZF1. These are still hooks, but you can now get greater flexibility if you want to by leveraging the capabilities of the EventManager. You will see examples of that later on.

Sessions and a Name Change

Note that the code inside dispatch is also different. Many components have undergone subtle name changes. In this example, \Zend\Session\Namespace is not possible because Namespace is a reserved word in PHP as of version 5.3. The replacement in this case is: \Zend\Session\Container, which we alias into our own namespace with use as SessionContainer.

Implicit versus Explicit

Singletons are mostly gone in ZF2. There is no registry, although you could use the Zend_Registry from ZF1 if you wanted to. The registry was a typical singleton. Singletons tend to get in the way of flexibility, and flexibility is key to ZF2. In this guide, I mention the EventManager and the ServiceManager frequently, as if they were omnipotent singletons. They are not.

The MVC uses a ServiceManager, an EventManager, and a shared EventManager (of which there is only one), but you can have your own EventManagers and ServiceManagers to keep a good separation of concerns in your domain logic. If you want to get anything done in ZF2, you must explicitly tell your application how you want it done. It is under your control. Remember that when things get difficult.

Chapter 4

Getting Started

What did we just do? We compared an event hook implementation between ZF1 and ZF2 without considering the application in its entirety. If you are like me, it is likely that you wish to follow along with this book while trying out some code. It is difficult to try the previous example because it is out of context. It is easy enough to add the event to the `IndexController` of a fresh ZF1 application.

But how will you know if the event triggered without running a debugger or echoing something from the session in a view? For ZF2, the whole picture is even harder to get because you are probably new to ZF2, and there are at least two approaches you could take. The easiest is to modify the `Application` module in the `ZendSkeletonApplication`, and the more elaborate approach is to create your own module and try it in there. The latter is the approach I'm going to walk you through because it will help you better understand the differences between ZF1 and 2.

First of all, I will show you two screens, the ZF1 application (Figure 4.1) and the ZF2 application (Figure 4.2), each showing the result of the `helloAction` in their own way.

FIGURE 4.1

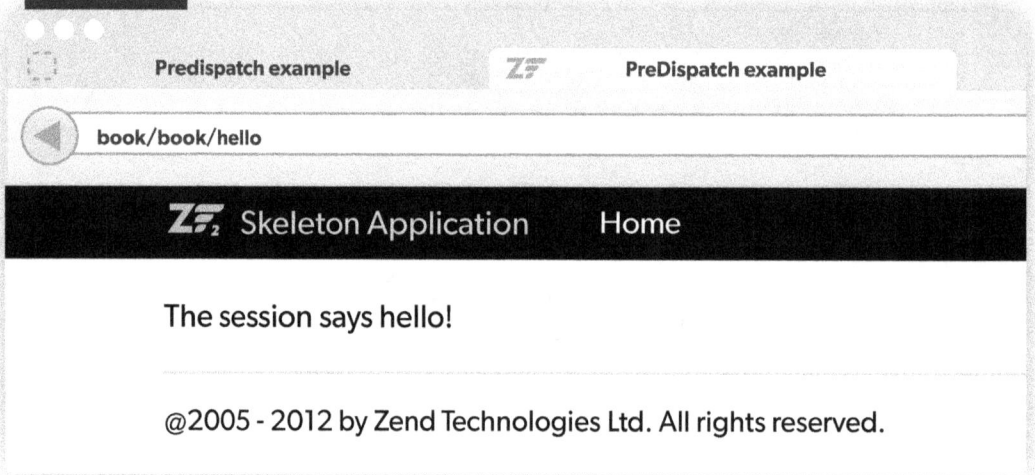

FIGURE 4.2

The `helloAction` is the action that demonstrates that we actually put something in the session. You can set (or add to) the page title from within the template like you could in ZF1:

```php
<?php
$this->headTitle(
    'PreDispatch example 2',
    Zend\View\Helper\PlaceHolder\Container\AbstractContainer::SET
);
?>
```

or simply

```php
<?php $this->headTitle('PreDispatch example 2', 'SET') ?>
```

Why Are the Screens Different?

When we migrate an application, we should not want to change its looks at the same time. If we do, we are in for trouble. It is best to make the change one step at a time. So why are these screens different? If we imagine we are doing a real migration, they should be identical. The answer is *layout*.

Note that this is not something you can replay from the code that accompanies the book. Once this code is shipped, the visual result of both helloAction should be the same.

Layouts

The reason that Figure 4.1 doesn't look exactly like Figure 4.2 is that the layouts are different. In fact, the ZF1 version doesn't even use a layout because a new ZF1 project, as created by Zend Tool, doesn't use a layout by default. The ZendSkeletonApplication, which, as you know, is the default ZF2 application, does use a layout. The code that produces the ZF1 screen is easy to explain.

The IndexController is shown in Listing 4.1. What you see in there is the default code generated by Zend_Tool plus the preDispatch hook and a helloAction method, which assigns the hello variable from the session to the view.

Listing 4.1 IndexController

```php
<?php
class IndexController extends Zend_Controller_Action
{
    public function preDispatch()
    {
        $session = new Zend_Session_Namespace('Fronted');
        $session->hello = 'The session says hello!';
    }

    public function init()
    {

    }

    public function indexAction()
    {
        // action body
    }

    public function helloAction()
    {
        $session = new Zend_Session_Namespace('Fronted');
        $this->view->hello = $session->hello;
    }
}
```

The corresponding view template is in Listing 4.2. This is an extremely simple view, which uses no layout. This is not realistic because in a real project, you will probably find yourself facing a complex layout, but for this example, it will do.

Listing 4.2 View template

```
<html>
<head>
    <title>Predispatch example</title>
</head>
<body>
<?php echo $this->hello ?>
</body>
</html>
```

Building Your Own Module

Because I follow the hard way of building my ZF2 module, implementing the dispatch event in ZF2 requires more work than just adding two functions and a view script. Here is a step-by-step guide to building your own very basic module next to the default Application module.

1. Create a directory Book at the same level as Application, under the module directory in the ZendSkeletonApplication.
2. Under Book, you create a directory structure, which you can mirror from Application. It is easy to write a small shell script that creates all these directories in one go so that you can automate the creation of future modules if you wish. Alternatively, you could try ZFTool. This structure is a recommendation because ZF2 will let you play your own game if you like. But I will stick to the recommendation.
3. Add a Module.php file that contains the Book\Module class. Note that your module always lives in its own namespace, which is named after the module.
4. Add the IndexController.
5. Add the hello.phtml view.
6. Activate the module by adding it in config/application.config.php.

If you build your own module like this, step by step, you will notice that certain parts are missing and that you have to copy certain parts of the default Application module to make it work. This way, you will learn quickly what parts are required and which aren't. Remember that the Module.php file is the only *real requirement* for a ZF2 module.

We will now go through the steps in more detail to identify exactly which parts we really need for our basic setup.

Don't Create a Module Called `Default`!

You can't have a module called `Default`. The first thing you would have to do if you edit the `Module.php` file is type `namespace Default;`. This is invalid in PHP because `default` is a reserved keyword (used in a `switch` statement).

The Module Directory and its Structure

The `Book` module directory is going to be created next to `module/Application`. In Figure 4.3, you can see the minimal basic structure needed to produce Figure 4.2, the output of the `helloAction`. What we see is very similar to the ZF1 project structure. One notable difference is the `src` directory under the `Book` module directory. It hosts the classes that belong to this module under the 'extra' `src/Book` directory.

```
▼ 📂 module                           ┌──────────────┐
   ▶ 📂 Application                    │  FIGURE 4.3  │
   ▼ 📂 Book                           └──────────────┘
      ▼ 📂 src
         ▼ 📂 Book
            ▼ 📂 Controller
                 🐘 IndexController.php
      ▼ 📂 view
         ▼ 📂 book
            ▼ 📂 index
                 🐘 hello.html
      🐘 Module.php
```

This looks more complicated than we would wish for. It is logical that we place our `IndexController` under `Book/Controller` because its fully qualified name is `Book\Controller\IndexController`, and therefore, it must live in `Book/Controller/IndexController.php` on the file system. Because we are already in the `Book` module directory, the extra `src/Book` path could have been omitted. The reason for this extra path is the fact that the `Book` directory has to be PSR-0 compliant in its role as a place for the class library of your module. If you're not already familiar with PSR-0, you can find out more information about PSR-0 at *http://www.php-fig.org/psr/psr-0/*

Simply put, `src/Book` may only contain classes belonging to the `Book` namespace. If you were to put your classes at the same level as your view directory under the top-level `Book` directory, this would not be true. That is the reason there is an extra `src` directory, which functions as a signal: *"Hey, your library goes in here."*

Next to the src directory, there is a view directory, where your view scripts live. Unlike in ZF1, there is no intermediate scripts directory below that, but there is the intermediate book directory, which is named after the module; you will find the directories matching the controller names, such as index, directly under the view/book directory. In view/book/index, we put our hello.phtml view script. This script can be the same as for ZF1. However, there is the layout in ZF2, which is absent in ZF1. We will dig into this shortly.

Activating the Book Module

Activating the Book module is really simple. Just open the file config/application.config.php in your editor, and add it to the modules array:

```php
<?php
return array(
    'modules' => array(
        'Application',
        'Book',
    ),
    //[...]
);
```

Making the Module Work

In order to work, the module still needs some configuration. As I covered previously, unlike a ZF1 application, a ZF2 application doesn't load our controller and view automatically at a certain URL. We can't, for example, go to /book/index/hello to see our helloAction at work. We need to configure all of that. This adds work on our side, but it also makes it explicit and puts us in control.

Module Initialization

If you want your module to listen to certain (MVC) events, the init method or the onBootstrap method are good candidates.

From the manual:

> You will see an example of using the init method when we implement module-specific layouts, and you will see an example of using the onBootstrap event handler when we implement our own exception strategy.

> *The init() method is called for every module implementing this feature, on every page request, and it should only be used for performing lightweight tasks, such as registering event listeners. Rob Allen has collected a list of all ZF2 events.* [1]

[1]   All ZF2 Events, *http://akrabat.com/zend-framework-2/a-list-of-zf2-events/*

Controller Configuration

The Module class can implement the getConfig() method to return all of the configuration in one go as an associative array. It can also implement some alternative functions to retrieve specific configuration sections. The advantage of implementing, for example:

```
getControllerConfig(\Zend\Di\ServiceLocatorInterface $serviceLocator)
```

Instead of providing the controllers key in the configuration array, is that you can use the service locator argument to get other services for you. You can then inject these into any of your controllers.

Alternatively, if you configure the controllers key, you can do the same thing only if you provide a factory per controller. The factory will get a ServiceManager argument on which you can call getServiceLocator(). In our simple example, this configuration is sufficient:

```
public function getControllerConfig(
    \Zend\Di\ServiceLocatorInterface $serviceLocator
)
{
    return array(
        'invokables' => array(
            'Book\Controller\Index' =>
            'Book\Controller\IndexController',
        ),
    );
}
```

We could have accomplished the same thing by setting the controllers key in the array returned from getConfig():

```
'controllers' => array(
    'invokables' => array(
        'Book\Controller\Index' =>
            'Book\Controller\IndexController',
    ),
);
```

An invokable in this context is something you can use without parameters, such as a class name that can be used to create an instance or a concrete instance object. If you want to instantiate your controller with some arguments, you would have to use a factory or a closure that acts as a factory. In such a case, you specify it under the factories key, instead of under invokables. As with invokables, it is possible to specify just the fully qualified name of the factory class.

Note that the lengthy index Book\Controller\Index is an alias chosen to avoid key naming conflicts between modules. It is the result of a naming convention, but if we would have chosen Our-SuperCool-Awesome-Controller, this key would have been just as valid.

Configuring the Route and View

From getConfig(), we return the route configuration and the view configuration for only this simple example:

```
public function getConfig()
{
    return array(
        'router' => array(
            'routes' => array(
                'hello' => array(
                    'type' => 'Zend\Mvc\Router\Http\Literal',
                    'options' => array(
                        'route'    => '/index/hello',
                        'defaults' => array(
                            'controller' => 'Book\Controller\Index',
                            'action'     => 'hello',
                        ),
                    ),
                )
            )
        ),
        'view_manager' => array(
            'template_path_stack' => array(
                __DIR__ . '/view',
            ),
        ),
    );
}
```

Note that the only thing we tell the view_manager is where to get our views, which we do by specifying the template_path_stack.

The route configuration is more complex, but it can provide you with the same options you had in ZF1 if you need them. Note that the controller that we have specified for our route is designated by the lengthy alias that we specified in the getControllerConfig() method. Because this is about migration and we have full control over the route, we can make it match the route we used in ZF1, which was the default for ZF1, /index/hello. You'd likely not be using such a route, but this proves that you can do a conversion while preserving your routes.

Configure the Class Loader

The last thing we need before our module will work is to configure autoloading, something we also do in Book\Module.

```
public function getAutoloaderConfig()
{
    return array(
        'Zend\Loader\StandardAutoloader' =>
        array(
            'namespaces' => array(
                __NAMESPACE__ =>
                __DIR__ . '/src/' . __NAMESPACE__,
            ),
        ),
    );
}
```

Note that we do not use the fast class map autoloader here. We use the StandardAutoloader, which is the easiest to use. All you need to do is give it an array of namespaces associated with the paths they are in. Of course, in order for this to work, the classes in your namespace must be named following the PSR-0 convention. You can see that you are free to place your module classes anywhere you like. All you have to do is change the path here. But of course, it is just as easy to stick to the recommendation.

Now we have covered everything that was needed to convert our preDispatch event and the corresponding action and view that demonstrate the result. Note that only three files are involved. And while the directory structure may seem confusing at first, we only have these three files to contend with:

- Book/src/Book/Controller/IndexController.php
- Book/view/index/hello.phtml
- Book/Module.php

In the chapter about layouts, we will take a closer look at why the two screens are different and how we can rectify that. Before we do, we need to look at how errors are displayed.

Chapter 5

Error Handling and Logging

No `ErrorController`

ZF2 is all about the explicit configuration of dependencies and events. Error handling is subject to that, as well. Error handling can be easily configured, but you have to know where. On the other side of the spectrum, where you want to be completely in control, you can implement your own exception strategy, and then it is completely up to you what you do with the exception.

Simple Migration Steps for Error Handling

If you just want to migrate an existing application, then think of it in terms of what you had in ZF1 and how it translates to ZF2. In ZF1, you had an `ErrorController`, and you could configure the application to display the exceptions—or not—by configuring `resources.frontController.params.displayExceptions`.

In your ErrorController, you could check the value of the displayExceptions parameter and display the exception or a friendly message. The setting would typically be turned on in the development environment through reading the environment variable APPLICATION_ENV. In ZF2, this is different. What you get are error templates, some configuration options, and, if you must, an ExceptionStrategy.

Error Templates

In ZF2, you can configure error templates. The view manager can be configured with two predefined keys, which may point to an alias defined in your template map. That is what the default Application module does. The keys point to different templates for 404 and 500 errors. This is convenient if you want to treat entering a wrong URL differently from an application error.

In ZF1, the error controller checked the type of the exception and printed a different response header and a different message for a route mismatch (404) or an application error (500). In addition, it would set the exception variable on the view if exceptions had to be displayed.

If you are building your own module and want to do without the Application module, you might want to copy the two templates and their configuration from the Application module so that you can build on them.

Configuring Error Templates

In the view_manager configuration key, configure these keys with templates that you will define in the template_map:

```
'not_found_template'       => 'error/404',
'exception_template'       => 'error/index',
```

And in the template_map, configure the templates with the same keys:

```
'error/404'     => __DIR__ . '/view/error/404.phtml',
'error/index'   => __DIR__ . '/view/error/index.phtml',
```

Now copy the error templates directory from the Application module into your own view directory, and you will no longer need your Application module for error handling.

To Use Error Translations or Not?

If you copy both templates from the Application module, you will either have to edit them to not use translations, or you'll have to enable translations (see the chapter about translations or look in the Application module to see how it's done). If you forget this and an exception is thrown, you will not see the actual exception but this one:

```
Fatal error: Uncaught exception 'Zend\I18n\Exception\
RuntimeException' with message 'Translator has not been set'.
```

Practical Migration of Error Handling

Here are a few possible scenarios:

- You are facing the task of migrating a large application, and time is running out.
- You can't be bothered with the details of intelligent ways to handle errors and all the differences between ZF1 and ZF2.
- You just want the errors handled the same way as before.
- You have created a beautiful 404 page to display a friendly message and search suggestions to the end user.

If any of these reflect how you feel, then you'll want to reproduce your ZF1 behavior in your ZF2 application. Now, I can't show you how to handle all the different scenarios, but I can show you how to reproduce in ZF2 what happened to an unmatched route in ZF1. If I point my browser at http://localhost/book1/n, it will display the page you see in Figure 5.1. This is the behavior you get when displayExceptions is turned on in application.ini and the route can't be matched. In this case, the route match looks for an NController, which is not defined.

FIGURE 5.1

An error occurred

Page not found

Exception information:

Message: Invalid controller specified (n)

Stack trace:

```
#0 /Users/bartmcleod/projects/Bug Fixes/library/Zend/Controller/Front.php(954): Zend_Contr
#1 /Users/bartmcleod/projects/Bug Fixes/library/Zend/Application/Bootstrap/Bootstrap.php(9
#2 /Users/bartmcleod/projects/Bug Fixes/library/Zend/Application.php(366): Zend_Applicatio
#3 /Users/bartmcleod/projects/book/public/index.php(26): Zend_Application->run()
#4 {main}
```

Request Parameters:

```
array (
  'controller' => 'n',
  'action' => 'index',
  'module' => 'default',
)
```

If we do the same in our ZF2 application, we get the result displayed in Figure 5.2. As you can see, no additional information is shown about an exception in ZF2 (if you read on, you will learn that there is no exception **at all** if the route is not matched). By default, you only get the user-friendly message.

This is almost the same page you would see in ZF1 but with exceptions turned off. Therefore, in order to get back the friendly behavior, all you have to do is overwrite 404.phtml with your old beautiful template. However, if your ZF1 ErrorController added logic that was consumed in your template, then you will have to move that logic to the template. If that's not possible or if it is (rightfully) considered a bad practice, then you should implement your own exception strategy.

FIGURE 5.2

A 404 error occurred

Page not found

Display Exceptions?

The error templates 404.phtml and index.phtml that ship with the Application module do check for $this->display_exceptions. You should use $this for template variables in ZF1 style, but that is not the point here. The point is that you should know where to configure this variable so that you can mimic the old setting from application.ini, which controlled displaying exceptions.

In the old days, you would set this to true for development and to false for production. In ZF2, you configure this under the 'view_manager' configuration key in the same place where you configure the error templates. It is best to only configure these in config/autoload/local.php so that these settings will never make it to your production environment (see the chapter about configuring environments):

```php
// only inside a local.php file
return array(
    'view_manager' => array(
        'display_exceptions'       => true,
        'display_not_found_reason' => true,
    ),
);
```

For demonstration purposes, I have created an exceptionAction in the IndexController of the Book module:

```
public function exceptionAction()
{
    throw new \DomainException("This is a mock exception [..]");
}
```

And I have added a route for it:

```
// inside 'routes' configuration key in Module::getConfig()
'exception' => array(
    'type' => 'Zend\Mvc\Router\Http\Literal',
    'options' => array(
        'route'    => '/exception',
        'defaults' => array(
            'controller' => 'Book\Controller\Index',
            'action'     => 'exception',
        ),
    ),
),
```

Now, if I go to http://localhost/book/exception, I get to see the exception and the stacktrace (see Figure 5.3).

FIGURE 5.3

An error occurred

An error occurred during execution; please try again later.

Additional information:

DomainException

File:

/Users/bartmcleod/git/ZendSkeletonApplication/module/Book/src/Book/Controller/IndexController.php:34

Message:

This is a mock exception for testing exceptions.

Stack trace:

```
#0 /Users/bartmcleod/git/ZF2/library/Zend/Mvc/Controller/AbstractActionController.php(83): Book\Contro
#1 [internal function]: Zend\Mvc\Controller\AbstractActionController->onDispatch(Object(Zend\Mvc\MvcEv
#2 /Users/bartmcleod/git/ZF2/library/Zend/EventManager/EventManager.php(460): call_user_func(Array, Ob
#3 /Users/bartmcleod/git/ZF2/library/Zend/EventManager/EventManager.php(204): Zend\EventManager\EventM
#4 /Users/bartmcleod/git/ZF2/library/Zend/Mvc/Controller/AbstractController.php(117): Zend\EventManage
#5 /Users/bartmcleod/git/ZendSkeletonApplication/module/Book/src/Book/Controller/IndexController.php(2
#6 /Users/bartmcleod/git/ZF2/library/Zend/Mvc/DispatchListener.php(114): Book\Controller\IndexControll
#7 [internal function]: Zend\Mvc\DispatchListener->onDispatch(Object(Zend\Mvc\MvcEvent))
#8 /Users/bartmcleod/git/ZF2/library/Zend/EventManager/EventManager.php(460): call_user_func(Array, Ob
#9 /Users/bartmcleod/git/ZF2/library/Zend/EventManager/EventManager.php(204): Zend\EventManager\EventM
#10 /Users/bartmcleod/git/ZF2/library/Zend/Mvc/Application.php(294): Zend\EventManager\EventManager->t
#11 /Users/bartmcleod/git/ZendSkeletonApplication/public/index.php(12): Zend\Mvc\Application->run()
#12 {main}
```

The result of opening the non-existent page /book/n is now as in Figure 5.4. It says that no exception is available. This is different from ZF1, where a route mismatch was an exception, as we saw earlier (see Figure 5.1). If you used to log this kind of exception and still need to, you should register a handler to the

FIGURE 5.4

A 404 error occurred

Page not found

The requested URL could not be matched by routing.

No exception available

MvcEvent::EVENT_DISPATCH_ERROR event and log it in there:

```
// in Module::onBootstrap(MvcEvent $e)
$eventManager->attach(
    MvcEvent::EVENT_DISPATCH_ERROR,
    function($e) use ($logger){
        $logger->err(
            'A route mismatch occured at '
            . $_SERVER['REQUEST_URI']
        );
    }
);
```

ExceptionStrategy

Behind the scenes, a Zend\Mvc\View\Http\ExceptionStrategy or a RouteNotFoundStrategy in the same namespace is used by default to decide what to do with an exception or a route mismatch. They have a method, setDisplayExceptions(), which is used to toggle exceptions, but for the RouteNotFoundStrategy, you will find the setDisplayNotFoundReason() method more useful. If you want to interact with the ExceptionStrategy, you can do so inside the onBootstrap event hook of the Module class:

```
// inside Module::onBootstrap(MvcEvent $e)
$exceptionStrategy = $e->getApplication()
    ->getServiceManager()
    ->get('ViewManager')
    ->getExceptionStrategy();
```

Now, this works for 500 errors, while for a 404, you would need the getRouteNotFoundStrategy() method. Please note that you will not need to interact with either strategy in most cases.

Simplest Error Template

Warning: The behavior described as follows only exists if you do not configure any of the above templates. Skip this part if you are simply using the `Application` module or if you have already configured your error templates.

If you do not need or want any of the clever customizations, you can place an empty `error.phtml` in any of the configured view paths, and your errors will be thrown like you expect them to be. Without this template, the only exception you will see is that the error template can't be found. It looks like this:

```
Unable to render template 'error'; resolver could not
resolve to a file.
```

> *To me, this really looks like a bug, but I spoke to the developers about it in IRC on #zftalk.dev, and they think of it as normal behavior. The line of thought is: "**If there is an exception, the error template will be rendered**". In my opinion, when the `error.phtml` default template file doesn't exist, the exception should be thrown as is. I suppose no one will even object when I change the code accordingly.*

This is how you configure an `error` template:

```
'view_manager' => array(
    'template_map' => array(
        'error' => __DIR__ . '/view/error.phtml',
    ),
),
```

Alternatively, placing `error.phtml` on one of the configured paths in the `view_path_stack` will do equally well. The behavior that causes this to happen is also defined in the default `ExceptionStrategy`. In the case of an event that has an exception, a response is created with a view model.

On the view model, the template is set to `error` if no other exception template is defined. So if you want your errors to be thrown as is, you should configure a simpler exception strategy for the view manager and register it with the `EventManager`. You might also want to do this if you need additional logic when handling errors.

Full Control Over Errors: `ExceptionStrategy`

There we go! You're the brave developer who wants to do his own thing. Very well then! Let's implement a custom exception strategy, which re-throws the exception as is when `displayExceptions` is configured as `true` and shows the default exception template otherwise.

If you implement your own exception strategy, you are completely free in how you handle bad situations in the execution life-cycle of your application. For the sake of simplicity, I have chosen that the only customization is re-throwing the exception if displayExceptions is true.

First of all, we'll create the simplest exception strategy we can think of:

```php
<?php
namespace Book;

use Zend\Mvc\View\Http\ExceptionStrategy
    as ZendExceptionStrategy;

class ExceptionStrategy extends ZendExceptionStrategy
{
    public function prepareExceptionViewModel(MvcEvent $e)
    {
        if ($this->displayExceptions()
            && $exception = $e->getError()
        ) {
            // re-throw the exception
            $exception = $e->getParam('exception');

            if ($exception instanceof \Exception) {
                throw($exception);
            }
        }
        // default behavior
        return parent::prepareExceptionViewModel($e);
    }
}
```

This is a new class in our Book module namespace that extends the default ExceptionStrategy. Now we need to configure this as our exception strategy.

One thing that people try is what you would expect from the dependency injection principles: the exception strategy is registered as a service, so what is expected is that you can provide your own service, instead:

```php
public function getServiceConfig()
{
    return array(
        'invokables' => array(
            'ExceptionStrategy' => 'Book\ExceptionStrategy',
        ),
    );
}
```

If you try this, you get the following exception:

```
Zend\ServiceManager\ServiceManager::setService: A service by
the name "ExceptionStrategy" or another alias already exists and
cannot be overridden. Please use an alternate name.
```

As you can see, this is not the way to go. The other obvious approach would be to set the exception strategy on the view manager in the onBootstrap event handler. This yields yet another error:

```
Call to undefined method Zend\Mvc\View\Http\ViewManager::
setExceptionStrategy().
```

So this is not the way to go, either.

The key to understanding how to do it is the concept of the Zend\EventManager\ListenerAggregateInterface. An exception strategy implements it. This interface is for self-registering events. These events will register at a higher priority (100) than common MvcEvents. That means that passing your own ExceptionStrategy to the EventManager will result in your own ExceptionStrategy being triggered before the default:

```
// in Module::onBootstrap(MvcEvent $e)
$serviceManager = $e->getApplication()->getServiceManager();

/* get the merged config
 * (of all modules, *.global.php and *.local.php)
 */
$config = $serviceManager->get('Config');

// instantiate the custom Book\ExceptionStrategy
$exceptionStrategy = new ExceptionStrategy();

// pass configuration options!
$exceptionStrategy->setDisplayExceptions(
    $config['view_manager']['display_exceptions']
)->setExceptionTemplate(
    $config['view_manager']['exception_template']
);

// attach the ListenerAggregateInterface
$eventManager->attachAggregate($exceptionStrategy);
```

Now, when display_exceptions is turned on and an exception is thrown, it just gets re-thrown.

Logging

If in ZF1, a logger was configured as a resource in `application.ini`, logging of errors used to be done in the `ErrorController`, which is now gone. This is what made the ZF1 default error logging mechanism tick: In the `ErrorController`, there was a function `getLog()` that would pull the logger from the automagically loaded resources:

```
// inside ErrorController:

public function getLog()
{
    $bootstrap = $this->getInvokeArg('bootstrap');
    if (!$bootstrap->hasResource('Log')) {
        return false;
    }
    $log = $bootstrap->getResource('Log');
    return $log;
}
```

After an exception occurred, the `indexAction` of the `ErrorController` would be called, and the error would be logged:

```
// inside errorController::indexAction

// Log exception, if logger available
if ($log = $this->getLog()) {
    $log->log(
        $this->view->message,
        $priority,
        $errors->exception
    );
    $log->log(
        'Request Parameters',
        $priority,
        $errors->request->getParams()
    );
}
```

In order to autoload the logger, it had to be configured as a resource in `application.ini`:

```
// log resource automagically loaded from application.ini
[development]
resources.log.firebug.writerName = "Firebug"
resources.log.firebug.filterName = "Priority"
resources.log.firebug.filterParams.priority = Zend_Log::INFO
```

It must be said that if you are converting a very old ZF1 application, then you will likely not see any auto-loaded resources, and the logger will be configured differently.

This is the output produced in production when going to /book1/exception where I purposely throw an exception:

```
// in application.log, configured for production
2013-04-22T07:41:46+02:00 CRIT (2): Application error
2013-04-22T07:41:46+02:00 CRIT (2): Request Parameters
```

Logging in ZF2

As you should now expect, in ZF2, logging has to be configured explicitly and is no longer tied to an ErrorController because we don't have one. However, logging errors has been made incredibly easy. You can log both PHP errors and exceptions by registering a logger instance using static methods on Zend\Log\Logger:

```
// near the top of Module.php
use Zend\Log\Logger;

// inside Module::onBootstrap(MvcEvent $e)
$logger = $serviceManager->get('Book\Log');
Logger::registerErrorHandler($logger);
Logger::registerExceptionHandler($logger);
```

And of course, you must then configure the Book\Log as a service. For the sake of the example, I use the FirePHP logger because that's my favorite. Alternatively, you can log errors to a file or a database.

> *FirePHP is a browser extension that enables you to log to your Firebug Console using a simple PHP method call. Originally developed for Firefox's Firebug extension, there's also a version available for Chrome.*

To use Zend Framework's FirePHP writer, you must first add the FirePHPCore Server Library. You can do this with composer by adding the following to your composer.json file:

```
"repositories": [{
    "type" : "pear",
    "url" : "pear.firephp.org",
    "vendor-alias" : "firephp"
}],
"minimum-stability": "dev",
"require" : {
    "firephp/FirePHPCore" : "*"
}
}
```

Then from within your module code:

```php
// near the top of Module.php
require_once 'vendor/FirePHPCore/FirePHP.class.php';

use Zend\Log\Writer\FirePhp as FirePhpWriter;
use Zend\Log\Writer\FirePhp\FirePhpBridge;

// in Module::getServiceConfig(), 'factories' key
'Book\Log' => function($serviceManager) {
    $log = new Logger();
    $writer = new FirePhpWriter(
        new FirePhpBridge(
            new \FirePHP()
        )
    );
    $log->addWriter($writer);
    return $log;
},
```

With this setup, you will see FirePHP log the exception that is thrown at
/book/exception (Figure 5.5).

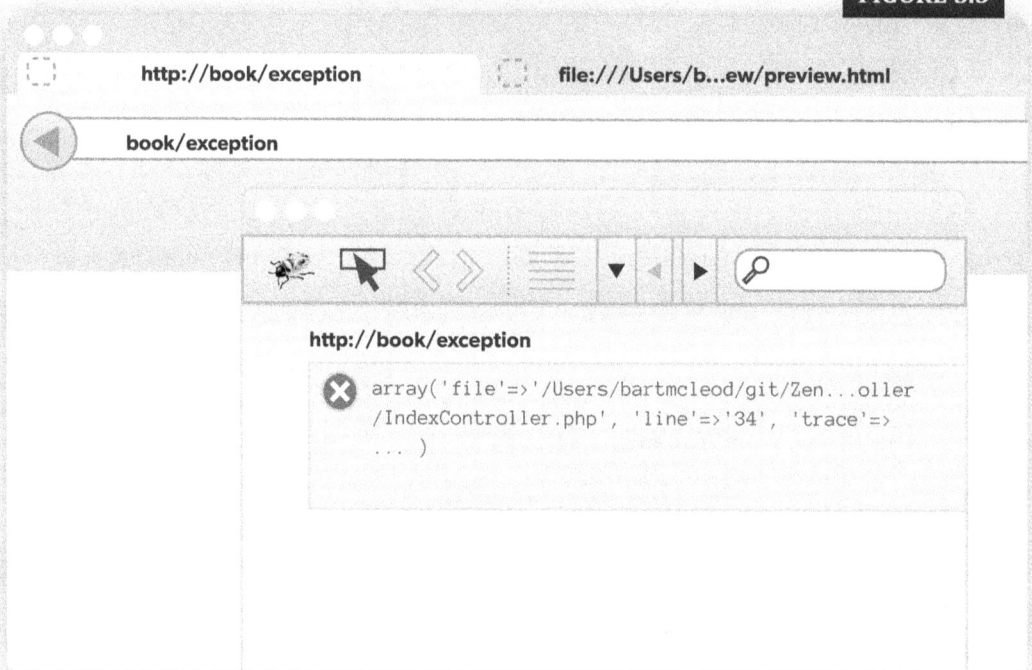

FIGURE 5.5

If you are curious to know why `vendor` is on the `include_path`, you should take a look inside `application.config.php` where it's configured.

In many scenarios, particulary apps with AJAX requests or one-page application logging with FirePHP to the browser can be very useful, It somehow gets in the way of the actual throwing of the exception, so the page doesn't show the exception being thrown anymore. I suppose it ends up somewhere in the headers just after spitting out the FirePHP headers, so it's probably better to try and catch the exception and then log it instead of trying to log it to some fancy Firefox extension while also throwing it, thus halting PHP execution and ending up with a response that is halfway finished. Your browser doesn't like that. You can use s `Zend\Log` instance with any number of Writers, so you should consider adding a Steam or Database writer as well.

Layout

Please take a look back at *Figure 5.1* and *5.2*. They show two screen shots taken from the ZF1 and ZF2 applications, respectively. They do not look the same, even though they should. This is due to the fact that I took the default, quick start, applications of both frameworks as my starting point. The ZF1 default application *does not* come with layout, while the ZF2 ZendSkeletonApplication *does*.

If you paid attention, you will have noticed that the configuration of our ZF2 Book module doesn't mention layout; it is the layout of the default Application module that we see in action. For the view script, I took the ZF1 view script and stripped out the *html*, *head*, *title*, and *body* tags because those are already included in the layout.

Changing the Default Layout

There are several approaches we can take to make the layouts the same between our ZF1 and ZF2 examples:

1. Disable the Application module in the ZF2 application (this will produce an error for several reasons).
2. Add layout to the ZF1 application, and add layout configuration to our ZF2 Book module. Then use the same layout template in both cases.
3. Configure the ZF2 Book module so that it no longer uses layout but, instead, uses the same view script we had for ZF1.
4. Disable layout in ZF2 only for the hello action.

While the first and last two options are interesting from an academic point of view, it is likely for a real-life project to use a layout, which would lead to the second option. The second option can be implemented in five ways if, in all five cases, we configure a layout for the Book module.

Here's how:

1. Load the Book module last (like we already do in application.config.php). This will overwrite the layout configuration of the default Application module, effectively giving both modules the same layout.
2. Disable—i.e., do not load—the Application module. This will automatically leave us with only the layout of the Book module.
3. Use module-specific layouts. This requires some extra programming. You will need it sooner or later, so I will show you how to do exactly this, with a lot of help from Evan Coury, who blogged about it.
4. Override the layout configuration in config/autoload/book.global.php. The only difference with the first option is that by doing it this way, the loading order of the modules doesn't matter because the configuration loaded from *.global.php overrides module configuration (more about that in the Configuration section).
5. Configure a layout key in the view_manager configuration to point to a layout template that we want to use. This is probably the simplest option.

Is Layout Required?

While it is academic, you might nevertheless be curious to know whether loading the default Application module would free us from the layout. It doesn't; it gives us an error, instead:

```
Unable to render template "layout/layout"
```

If you disable the Application module *without* configuring your error template(s) at the same time, you will see a different error:

```
Unable to render template 'error'; resolver could not
resolve to a file
```

In the chapter about *error templates*, you can read about how to solve this.

Apparently, while ZF2 is very flexible and explicit, a layout is implicitly enabled. Can we turn it off at all? The answer is yes. In fact, Abdul Malik Iksan blogged about it [1], and I have simplified his code to show you how it can be done for a module:

```
public function onBootstrap(\Zend\Mvc\MvcEvent $e)
{
    $sharedEvents = $e
        ->getApplication()
        ->getEventManager()
        ->getSharedManager();
    $sharedEvents->attach(
        __NAMESPACE__,
        'dispatch',
        function ($e) {
            $result = $e->getResult();
            $result->setTerminal(true);
        }
    );
}
```

The key in this example, which is a good demonstration of how events can be used, is the line `$result->setTerminal(true);`. This will make only the view script render, not the layout.

Disabling layout by setting `terminal` to `true` on the result of the dispatch event can be used at any level: *per action*, *per module* (as shown above) and *per application*. In the action, you can also set this on the view model (the view model in that case is also the result of the dispatch action, but it could equally be a response object).

Module-Specific Layouts

What we really want are module-specific layouts. Let's assume that we have an admin area and a front end, and we don't want them to share their layouts. While the event manager is module agnostic, we can use the module *namespace* to detect which module we are in and use that to decide which layout to render.

In order for this to work, you should configure a key for a layout template for each module that needs a specific layout:

```
'view_manager' => array(
    'template_map' => array(
        'layout/book'
        => __DIR__ . '/../view/layout/layout.phtml',
    ),
),
```

[1]   Zend Framework 2 : Disable Layout in specific Module, *http://wp.me/p2Eg2-un*

This only means that the path to the template can now be found using the layout/book key. Nothing else. This will *not* automatically make the Book module render this layout.

Layouts are rendered by default when configured with the *layout/layout* key. If you want to use a different key, you can do so by configuring the layout key inside the view_manager configuration with your own layout key:

```
'view_manager' => array(
    'layout' => 'layout/book',
)
```

This will still not be module specific: all of your modules will now use this layout.

You should remember that configuration is stacked and merged. So if in the template_map configuration, you use layout/layout as the key for the layout view script path, it would work but only if your module was registered last in application.config. And then, if it is listed last and you use the layout/layout key, all of your modules will use the admin layout, which is obviously not what we intended to happen.

While there is no module awareness, there is an awareness of the topmost namespace being dispatched. Evan Coury, one of the hard-working community members developing ZF2, wrote a great blog post about this[2]. I used the example in his post to make my module-specific layouts work.

It works like this; in the Module.php file where your Module class lives, you use the init method to register for an event which is specific to dispatching the controllers that live in the module for which you want to use a specific layout:

```
public function init(ModuleManager $moduleManager)
{
    // from the example by Evan Coury
    $sharedEvents = $moduleManager
        ->getEventManager()
        ->getSharedManager();
    $sharedEvents->attach(
        __NAMESPACE__,
        'dispatch',
        function($e) {
            // specific to namespace
            $controller = $e->getTarget();
            // set layout alias
            $controller->layout('layout/mylayout');
        },
        100);
}
```

[2]   *http://blog.evan.pro/module-specific-layouts-in-zend-framework-2*

What is done in this code is that if anything (more specifically: a controller) is dispatched in our namespace, we want to change the layout. Controllers implement the `Dispatchable` interface, and the request is dispatched to them at dispatch time, so that is also a good time to set the layout. The priority is set to 100 in this example, but the simple examples work equally well if you omit this.

The first argument of the `attach` method is a context identifier for the event, which limits the effect of the trigger to a certain context. In case you are wondering who is firing the dispatch event in a context named `__NAMESPACE__`, this is what Evan answers:

> What we did was add the first level of the namespace of the controller being dispatched as an event identifier in the AbstractActionController. In fact, it is done in its parent class, `AbstractController`:

```
public function setEventManager(
    EventManagerInterface $events)
{
    $events->setIdentifiers(array(
        'Zend\Stdlib\DispatchableInterface',
        __CLASS__,
        get_called_class(),
        $this->eventIdentifier,
        /* [LOOK: this is where it happens!!] */
        substr(
            get_called_class(),
            0,
            strpos(get_called_class(), '\\')
        )
    ));
    $this->events = $events;
    $this->attachDefaultListeners();

    return $this;
}
```

With Evan's solution in place, our `Module.php` file now looks like Listing 6.1. Of course, in order to make our book layout work, we had to add a directory named `layout` to our view directory and add the `book.phtml` layout script in there.

Listing 6.1 Module with a specific layout

```php
<?php
namespace Book;
use Zend\ModuleManager\ModuleManager as ModuleManager;
use Zend\Di\ServiceLocatorInterface;

class Module
{
    public function init(ModuleManager $moduleManager)
    {
        // from example by Evan Coury
        $sharedEvents = $moduleManager
            ->getEventManager()
            ->getSharedManager();
        $sharedEvents
            ->attach(
                __NAMESPACE__,
                'dispatch',
                function($e) {
                    // specific to namespace
                    $controller = $e->getTarget();
                    // now you can use a different key!
                    $controller->layout('layout/book');
                },
                100
            );
    }

    public function getConfig()
    {
        return array(
            'router' => array(
                'routes' => array(
                    'hello' => array(
                        'type' => 'Zend\Mvc\Router\Http\Literal',
                        'options' => array(
                            'route'    => '/index/hello',
                            'defaults' => array(
                                'controller'
                                        => 'Book\Controller\Index',
                                'action' => 'hello',
                            ),
                        ),
                    )
                )
            ),
```

```php
        'view_manager' => array(
            'template_path_stack' => array(
                __DIR__ . '/view',
            ),
        ),
    );
}

public function getControllerConfig(
    ServiceLocatorInterface $serviceLocator = null)
{
    return array(
        'invokables' => array(
            'Book\Controller\Index'
                => 'Book\Controller\IndexController',
        ),
    );
}

public function getAutoloaderConfig()
{
    return array(
        'Zend\Loader\StandardAutoloader' => array(
            'namespaces' => array(
                __NAMESPACE__ => __DIR__ . '/src/'
                                 . __NAMESPACE__,
            ),
        ),
    );
}

/**
 * @param \Zend\Mvc\MvcEvent $e
 */
/* This is an example of how to not render layout
   per module, which we do not use
public function onBootstrap(\Zend\Mvc\MvcEvent $e)
{
    $sharedEvents = $e->getApplication()
                    ->getEventManager()
                    ->getSharedManager();
    $sharedEvents->attach(
        __NAMESPACE__,
        'dispatch',
        function ($e) {
            $result = $e->getResult();
            $result->setTerminal(true);
        }
    );
}
*/
}
```

The contents of the layout script are almost as they would be in ZF1:

```php
<?php echo $this->docType('HTML5') ?>

<head>
    <?php echo $this->headMeta()->setCharset('utf-8') ?>

    <?php echo $this->headTitle() ?>

</head>
<body>
<?php echo $content ?>
</body>
</html>
```

The main difference is that in ZF1, we would have written $this->layout()->content, instead of $content, so this has become a little easier.

Chapter

7

The View

We already know that view scripts have improved, as you no longer need to type $this-> in front of view variables. You can use them as local variables. Let's look at the following edge case (I have seen many views in ZF1 applications with code like this).

```php
<?php
// variable $products instantiated in view script
$products = array('apples', 'bananas');

// $this->products assigned to view in controller action
foreach ($this->products as $product) {
    // do something
}
```

In ZF2, $this->products and $products are the same if products is returned in the view model, while in ZF1, they are different. However, in ZF2, as soon as we assign a new value to $products, it is different from $this->products. They are not references to each other. This is true at least for a scalar value, where objects would be references at all times, unless you clone them. The following view script has the same output in ZF1 and ZF2 if $this->products holds the value array('orange', 'kiwi'):

```
<h1>Products</h1>
<?php
    $products = array('apple', 'banana');
?>
<?php echo $this->htmlList($this->products) ?>
<?php echo $this->htmlList($products) ?>
```

The output is:

```
<h1>Products</h1>
<ul>
    <li>orange</li>
    <li>kiwi</li>
</ul>
<ul>
    <li>apple</li>
    <li>banana</li>
</ul>
```

In ZF2, we do not assign the value of products to the view, like we did in ZF1. Instead, we return a view model or an associative array from the controller action. There are **three** ways to do this. In ZF1, there were **two** ways of assigning variables to the view. You must take care to check for both ways when you do a migration. The two ways of ZF1 looked like this:

```
// assigning to the view object from inside
// the controller action
$this->view->products = array('orange', 'kiwi');
```

or

```
// pass an array of vars via assign()
$vars = array('products' => array('orange', 'kiwi'));
$this->view->assign($vars);
```

These two ways could be mixed.

In ZF2, the three ways are the following:

```
public function productsAction()
{
    // returning an array of view variables
    // from a controller action
    return array('products' => array('orange', 'kiwi'));
}
```

or

```
use Zend\View\Model\ViewModel;

// returning a ViewModel object containing view
// variables specified in the constructor
return new ViewModel(
    array('products' => array('orange', 'kiwi'))
);
```

or

```
// returning a ViewModel object containing view
// variables assigned as needed in program flow.
$view = new ViewModel();
$view->products = array('orange', 'kiwi');
return $view;
```

Modifying the `ViewModel`

In addition to what you could do in ZF1, you can modify the view model to alter the behavior of the view. As we saw earlier with layout, if you do *not* want to render the layout for a specific action, but only the view script itself, you can use the `setTerminal()` method on your view model:

```
$view->setTerminal(true);
```

Render a Different Template

By default, the template being rendered is named after the action. The `helloAction` renders the `hello.phtml` template. In ZF1, you could do the following inside the controller action in order to render a template with a different name:

```
// render the form.phtml template from the helloAction
$this->render('form');
```

In ZF2, you set a different template on the view model to achieve the same:

```
// render the hello template from the productsAction
$view->setTemplate('book/index/hello.phtml');
```

template_path_stack and template_map

In the above case, the view directory is on the template path stack (see the view_manager configuration), but you still need to specify the path from there to the alternative template. If you have configured an alias for a template, that works, too. For example, I can add an alias for an alternative products view script, using the template_map key in the configuration of the view_manager:

```
// inside 'view_manager' configuration array
'template_map' => array(
    'products' => __DIR__
                . '/view/book/index/alternative.phtml',
),
```

Now, I can change the view model inside the products action so that it will render this alternative view script:

```
// use the alias 'products' in the controller action
$view->setTemplate('products');
```

By the way, using a template_map is faster than relying on the template_path_stack because it doesn't require any searching the filesystem.

Nested View Models vs. Partials

Nested view models are a novelty of ZF2. How do these relate to partials, and when do we need to consider nested view models over partials in a migration process? Let's create an example that uses a partial in ZF1 and see what we can do in ZF2. So in the book ZF1 application, we put a partialAction method in the IndexController and make it use a the-partial.phtml. The partial.phtml action template looks like this:

```
<h1>View script using a partial</h1>
<?php
    echo $this->partial(
        'index/partials/the-partial.phtml',
        array('variable' => 'Got a variable!')
    )
?>
```

And the partial itself, `view/scripts/index/partials/the-partial.phtml`:

```
<h2>Partial</h2>
<p>This is the partial.</p>
<p>
    <?php echo $this->variable ?>
</p>
```

FIGURE 7.1

This is the ZF 1 layout (/Users/bartmcleoud/project/book/application/layouts/layout.phtml)

View script using partial

Partial

This is partial.

Got a variable!

The result for ZF1 can be seen in Figure 7.1. The good news is that this can be reused in almost the same way in ZF2. The only thing that might need a change is the path to the partial, as your view paths may be different. Of course, you could modify the view path configuration and not change a single line in the templates. In our example application, I did change the path in `partial.phtml`:

```
<h1>View script using a partial</h1>
<?php
    echo $this->partial(
        'book/index/partials/the-partial.phtml',
        array('variable' => 'Got a variable!')
    )
?>
```

The only change is that the module name and a slash are prefixed to the path (`book/`). This is because the `view` directory is in the configured view paths, and the `book` directory is found in there, so we can start the path starting with the `book` directory.

Now can we get the same results using a nested view model? Inside the nestedAction in ZF2, we set up the view models:

```
public function nestedAction()
{
    $partialView = new ViewModel();
    $partialView->setTemplate(
        'book/index/partials/the-partial.phtml'
    );
    $partialView->variable = 'Nested model has a variable!';

    $view = new ViewModel();
    $view->addChild($partialView, 'nested');
    return $view;
}
```

The second argument to addChild is the variable name that the output of the nested view will get in the parent template. The nested.phtml is therefore very simple:

```
<h1>View script using nested model</h1>
<?php
    echo $nested
?>
```

A route must be defined for the nested action, but after that, it works seamlessly. The main difference is that in ZF2, it's easier to control complex structures when building nested view models inside your controller than it is to keep track of nested partials and partial loops from within your views. This makes it easier to keep controlling logic where it belongs: inside your controller.

Modifying the Layout

The layout is just another view model to which your action view model is added, like when you nest view models yourself. That means that if you retrieve the layout within your controller action or within your view template, you can do things like alter the layout template or insert additional view models into the layout. Getting the layout inside your controller action is straightforward:

```
$layout = $this->layout();
```

The ZF2 manual has excellent sections on the view layer, so I'm not going to repeat that information here. Please remember that if you have advanced needs, the manual is the place to read about the new and cool features available. Make sure you bookmark *http://framework.zend.com/manual/current/en/modules/zend.view.quick-start.html*.

Escaping Variables

Automatic escaping of view variables is another new feature in ZF2. In the case of a conversion, you would have to remove all current calls to `$this->escape($this->someparam)` and replace them by just $someparam. Converting is complicated, however, by the fact that object properties and array elements are not automatically escaped.

These must be escaped by calling:

```
$this->escapeHtml($someparam['some-element'])
```

or:

```
$this->escapeHtml($someparam->someProperty)
```

Note that `$this->escape` won't work anymore.

The view helpers that help you escape now depend on the output context, and you should call the appropriate helper for the context you are escaping to. In this case, I assumed HTML as the context. The new helpers are EscapeUrl, EscapeCss, EscapeHtml, EscapeHtmlAttr, and EscapeJs. Most of the replacement work can be done by a *replace in files* using a regular expressions. Of course, if you want a quick and easy way, you could also write your own Escape view helper that returns `$this->view->escapeHtml($value)`.

View Helpers

In ZF1, view helpers had a method named after the last part of their name, and this method would invoke the view helper. For example, Zend_View_Helper_Url would have the url() method. That method could return either a string or the object itself. In the latter case, an additional __toString() method was needed to return the string output from the view helper.

Simple view helpers do not need that, but more complex ones do. This mechanism still works in ZF2, but the method that is used to invoke the view helper can't have the same name. Consider the URL view helper as an example. Its fully qualified name would be Zend\View\Helper\Url, and with namespaces, it would have the class declaration listed below. However, because of backwards compatibility, the url method would be considered a constructor, so it shouldn't be used as an alias to invoke the helper.

```
namespace Zend\View\Helper;

// this doesn't work as in ZF1
class Url extends \Zend\View\Helper\AbstractHelper {
    // [...]
    public function url()
    {
        // [...]
    }
}
```

function url() would be seen as the constructor because the name is the same as the class name; therefore, this had to change. ViewHelpers now implement the __invoke() magic method from the PHP documentation[1]

The __invoke() method is called when a script tries to call an object as a function.

ViewHelpers may extend Zend\View\Helper\AbstractHelper or implement setView and getView methods, thus implementing the Zend\View\Helper\HelperInterface. An example is in Listing 7.1.

Listing 7.1 Implementing `HelperInterface`

```php
<?php
namespace Book\View\Helper;
use Zend\View\Helper\HelperInterface;
use Zend\View\Renderer\RendererInterface as Renderer;

class Hello implements HelperInterface
{
    protected $view;

    public function __invoke()
    {
        return 'Hello from ViewHelper Hello!';
    }

    public function setView(Renderer $view)
    {
        $this->view = $view;
    }

    public function getView()
    {
        return $this->view;
    }
}
```

[1]   http://php.net/manual/en/language.oop5.magic.php#object.invoke

Unless you have a specific reason, it is simpler to just extend the `AbstractHelper` (Listing 7.2).

Listing 7.2 Extending `AbstractHelper`

```php
<?php
namespace Book\View\Helper;
use Zend\View\Helper\AbstractHelper;

class HelloSimple extends AbstractHelper
{
    public function __invoke()
    {
        return 'Simple hello from ViewHelper HelloSimple!';
    }
}
```

Configuring Your View Helpers

In ZF1, your view helpers had to be placed in the `view/helpers` directory, and they would be found automatically. You could configure this otherwise, but in ZF2, you *have* to configure your view helpers explicitly. Configuration of view helpers can be simple, though:

```php
'view_helpers' => array(
    'invokables' => array(
        'hello' => 'Book\View\Helper\Hello',
    ),
),
```

Note that the `view_helpers` key goes at the top level of the configuration array returned from `getConfig()` (*not* under `view_manager`). Alternatively, you might implement the `getViewHelperConfig()` method in `Module` to return the same array.

Either way, you are not limited to configuring `invokables`. You may also configure `factories` as a class name, as a closure, or as a concrete instance of a factory. The first argument of the factory method is a `Zend\View\HelperPluginManager` instance, on which you can call `getServiceLocator()`. The service locator that is returned can get you any service configured for the application. So this is a good way to inject dependencies into you view helper, should you need any.

Caching and Closures Don't Mix

The advantage of *not* using closures as factories in your configuration anywhere is that you will be able to cache your configuration because your configuration will be serializable. Because closures have an in-memory state and cannot provide a __sleep or a __wakeup method, they can't be restored from a cached string representation. Writing closures, on the other hand, is easy and straightforward. In general, it is recommended that you write factory classes, instead, and provide the class names to your factories configuration.

An example of a view helper that needs a dependency (a logger) is the Logger view helper in Listing 7.3.

Listing 7.3 View helper with a dependency

```php
<?php
namespace Book\View\Helper;

use Zend\View\Helper\AbstractHelper;

class Logger extends AbstractHelper
{
    protected $logger;

    public function __invoke($message)
    {
        $this->logger->info($message);
    }

    public function setLogger($logger)
    {
        $this->logger = $logger;
    }
}
```

We can configure this using a closure like this:

```php
'view_helpers' =>  array(
    'factories' => array(
        'logger' => function(HelperPluginManager $pm) {
            $sm = $pm->getServiceLocator();
            $logger = $sm->get('Book\Log');
            $viewHelper = new View\Helper\Logger();
            $viewHelper->setLogger($logger);
            return $viewHelper;
        }
    ),
),
```

As you can see, the logger dependency is injected into the view helper when the view helper is requested from the closure. You may have view helpers in your ZF1 project that have many dependencies. By configuring those dependencies as a service with the service manager, you can inject them into your view helper at creation time.

Autoloading Your View Helper

You may wonder how the view helper is found once it has been configured as shown above. Book is the module namespace, and the path to the module classes is configured in the Book\Module class that is defined in the obligatory Module.php file inside the Book module directory. The function getAutoloaderConfig (Listing 7.4) returns the configuration for the autoloaders, and in this case, the StandardAutoloader is the one that finds the view helper class located at module/Book/src/Book/View/Helper/Hello.php.

Listing 7.4 Autoloader configuration

```
public function getAutoloaderConfig()
{
    return array(
        'Zend\Loader\StandardAutoloader' => array(
            'namespaces' => array(
                __NAMESPACE__ => __DIR__ . '/src/'
                    . __NAMESPACE__,
            ),
        ),
    );
}
```

Of course, you can configure this any way you like, but it is probably best to stick to conventions and established best practices. One of the things you would want to do in production is to configure a class map autoloader, instead, because it is faster.

The View has Grown Up with ZF2

The View layer has grown up with ZF2. In fact, it is so flexible that it is almost dazzling to read the documentation. Try it for yourself: *http://framework.zend.com/manual/2.0/en/modules/zend.view.quick-start.html*. The whole view-rendering process has been made so that you can configure it completely tailored to your needs. If you had to play tricks in your ZF1 application to generate specific responses or sophisticated layouts, you should definitely get a profound understanding of the new view layer before you migrate. You will find something useful in there, which may lead to a more robust or better-performing application than you had before.

Chapter 8

Controller Plugins & Translations

Action Helpers

Action helpers were not widely used in ZF1. I have seen several applications that didn't implement any action helpers when they could have. An action helper should not be confused with Zend_View_Helper_Action, the latter being a view helper that calls an action on a controller.

Action helpers were a means to share code snippets, a bit like traits, between controllers, that had little in common otherwise. One of the things that kept me puzzled while learning ZF2 was, "Where did the action helpers go?" The answer is that they are now called *Controller Plugins*, and they are surprisingly easy to implement, configure, and use.

Before you look at implementing your own controller plugin, make sure to take a look at those already defined. In the sample ZF1 application called book, I have defined a useless action helper, purely for demonstration purposes:

```
// ZF1
class Book_Action_Helper_Name
    extends Zend_Controller_Action_Helper_Abstract
{
    public function direct()
    {
        $controller = $this->getActionController();
        return get_class($controller);
    }
}
```

It returns the class name of the controller. Notice how it implements a direct() method to allow calling it by its class name inside a controller. This action helper is consumed in the IndexController::nameAction action:

```
// ZF1
public function nameAction()
{
    $this->view->controllerName = $this->_helper->Name();
}
```

Note the underscore for the protected _helper property. The use of underscores is discouraged, and you should not do it in a ZF2 project. When we call Name() on this property, which holds the helper broker, it will look for an action helper that matches the configured naming rules and will then call the direct() method on it. The naming rules must be configured or set in the code. In the example application, they are configured in application.ini:

```
resources.frontController.actionhelperpaths.Book_Action_Helper \
    = APPLICATION_PATH "/controllers/helpers"
```

A ZF2 Controller Plugin

The above action helper from ZF1 can be replaced with a controller plugin:

```php
<?php
namespace Book\Controller\Plugin;

use Zend\Mvc\Controller\Plugin\AbstractPlugin;

class Name extends AbstractPlugin
{
    public function __invoke()
    {
        $controller = $this->getController();
        return get_class($controller);
    }
}
```

Configuring Controller Plugins

Configuring controller plugins is easy:

```php
// inside array returned by Module::getConfig():

'controller_plugins' => array(
    'invokables' => array(
        'controllerName' => 'Book\Controller\Plugin\Name',
    )
),
```

Consuming a Controller Plugin

Using a controller plugin inside a controller action is even easier than configuring it:

```php
public function nameAction()
{
    return array(
        'controllerName' => $this->controllerName(),
    );
}
```

The above snippet will expose the $controllerName variable to the view so that we can now reuse the name.phtml template from the ZF1 application. We *need* to configure a route for the name action in order to see the result (see "Configuring the route and view").

While we can reuse the template, we won't because we want to set a different title from within the template:

```
// name.phtml
<?php echo $controllerName ?>
<?php
    $this->headTitle('Controller Plugin example');
?>
```

Translations

Translations are not a requirement for your application to work, but many real-life ZF1 applications make use of translations. Not only can translations be used to translate from one language to another, but given their nature, they are also very handy when you want to translate column names or error codes to human-readable labels. It is therefore very likely that when migrating a ZF1 application, you will also have to migrate the translations.

CSV Format is Gone

There is no longer support for the *.csv format for your translations. I liked that format, but I'm probably one of the very few. It is, however, easy to convert your *.csv files to PHP arrays (which *are* supported—even recommended—for speed). You can convert either at runtime or just once, when you migrate the application. You can use file() to read your CSV file and get it back as an array of lines and then use str_getcsv to get the translation data on that line:

```
<?php
$translations = array();
$lines = file(__DIR__ . '/' . $locale . '.csv');

foreach ($lines as $line) {
    $pair = str_getcsv($line, ';');
    $translations[$pair[0]] = $pair[1];
}

return $translations;
```

The above example will convert a *.csv file for a given locale at runtime, but it's easy to use it for a one-off conversion. Doing it at runtime can be employed if you want to continue editing your translation in *.csv files.

Translations in ZF2

You will need to set up translations if you want to use the error templates (see the chapter about *error templates*) from the Application module without using the Application module itself. This is obviously doing things the hard way, but you will gain a better understanding of how they really work.

Even if you do not translate anything, you can still configure and build in a translation mechanism. If, one day, you decide you want it, it will already be in place.

The translator itself is configured at the root level of the configuration array returned from Module::getConfig():

```
'translator' => array(
    'locale' => 'nl_NL',
    'translation_file_patterns' => array(
      array(
          'type'     => 'PhpArray',
          'base_dir' => __DIR__ . '/language',
          'pattern'  => '%s.php',
      ),
    ),
),
```

In this configuration, it is clear that a default locale is specified (in my case, nl_NL), and translation_file_patterns specifies how the translation file can be found. The %s in the pattern will be replaced by the locale. So in my case, I write my translations in a file named nl_NL.php and place it in Book/language, where Book is the module directory.

As for the contents of the translations file, this is really simple, just like you could do it in ZF1:

```
<?php
return array(
    'An error occurred' => 'Er is een fout opgetreden',
);
```

As you can see, I have only translated a single string. You will see this in action at the URL /exception of the ZF2 sample application if you switch display_exceptions to false in config/autoload/local.php.

The service that provides the translator is configured in the service configuration. This can be either under the service_manager key in the root of the same main configuration array or in the dedicated Module::getServiceConfig() method:

```php
public function getServiceConfig()
{
    return array(
        'factories' => array(
            'translator' =>
            'Zend\I18n\Translator\TranslatorServiceFactory',
        ),
    );
}
```

Chapter 9

Forms

Zend\Form is a complete rewrite of Zend_Form. You won't find much that is backwards compatible in there. Compared to its predecessor, Zend\Form offers a clear separation of concerns. As a consequence, filtering and validating form values have been separated out into Zend\InputFilter. Zend\InputFilter takes care of both filtering and validating, while displaying forms is taken care of by a set of dedicated view helpers found in the Zend\Form\View\Helper namespace.

With Zend Framework 1, you could use Zend_Form in two ways, depending on whether you liked the decorator system. In the former case, you would only use very few decorators (the View_Helper being the absolute minimum). In the latter case, you might even have built your own decorator management system, like I did (sigh).

Decorators are Gone

If you don't know how the decorator system worked, don't worry; many did not, and the decorators are *gone* in ZF2. If you have to do a migration, you should avoid learning how to use decorators just to do the migration. Instead, focus on the desired end result: what your form should look like and what it should do.

Although I was one of the people who actually liked the challenges that came with using decorators, it would not be fair to only address a migration scenario based on the extensive use of decorators. So the example that I will show is a simple form that doesn't use any decorators other than the ones provided by default.

A Simple Form

First, I will create the form in my ZF1 application, then migrate it to ZF2. In the ZF1 example application, I have dedicated a controller to forms, and it is called FormController. The indexAction builds the simple form and renders it using the default view script located at /views/scripts/form/index.phtml. The index action:

```
public function indexAction()
{
    $form = new Zend_Form('person');
    $form->setAction($this->view->url());
    $form->addElement(
        'text','firstname', array('label' => 'First name')
    );
    $form->addElement(
        'text','lastname', array('label' => 'Last name')
    );
    $form->addElement(
        'submit', 'save', array('label' => 'Send')
    );
    $this->view->form = $form;
}
```

And the corresponding view script:

```
<?php echo $this->form ?>
```

This is all you needed in ZF1 to get the output in Listing 9.1. This is only the output of the form; I have omitted the layout in this case for clarity. As we can see, the form automatically renders <dl>, <dd>, and <td> tags, which many of us hated so much when we first met Zend_Form. Those who understood the power of the decorator system and learned to love it still needed quite some time to become proficient with it.

Listing 9.1 Decorated form in ZF1

```
<form enctype="application/x-www-form-urlencoded"
    action="/Form" method="post">
    <dl class="zend_form">
        <dt id="firstname-label">
            <label for="firstname" class="optional">
            First name</label>
        </dt>
        <dd id="firstname-element">
            <input type="text" name="firstname"
             id="firstname" value="" />
        </dd>
        <dt id="lastname-label">
            <label for="lastname" class="optional">
            Last name</label>
        </dt>
        <dd id="lastname-element">
            <input type="text" name="lastname"
             id="lastname" value="" />
        </dd>
        <dt id="save-label"> </dt>
        <dd id="save-element">
            <input type="submit" name="save"
             id="save" value="Send" />
        </dd>
    </dl>
</form>
```

Although it is unlikely that you are using Zend_Form without any customization, this form allows me to demonstrate some migration steps you could take.

The Route to Our Form

For starters, the URL where the form is displayed should be identical: in my case /book1/Form (ZF1) should translate to /book/Form (ZF2). Also, in order to keep a similar level of organization, I should create a dedicated FormController in my ZF2 Book module.

Note that it is disputable if the URL should be the same or not. ZF2 is modular by nature, and the modular structure can also provide a namespace for URLs. In that sense, it would be more logical to create the URL /book/Book/Form, thus including the Book module namespace in the URL. It is only because I want to demonstrate that you can create identical functionality with ZF2 compared to ZF1 that I insist on getting the form at the same URL as before.

In ZF1, the route /Form worked by default because I had a FormController, and I used the indexAction to display the form (index is the default, so you don't have to type /Form/index). In my ZF2 application, this won't work out of the box. There is a fallback route defined in the Application module, which follows the same pattern as in ZF1. But that will only work for the Application module because it is defined as a child route of the basic route /application defined in there. Still, all these routes would still be prefixed with /application, thus providing a namespace for all fallback routes in the application module.

A Custom Route

To keep things explicit, I will define a custom, literal route to the form.

```
'form' => array(
    'type' => 'Zend\Mvc\Router\Http\Literal',
    'options' => array(
        'route'    => '/Form',
        'defaults' => array(
            'controller' => 'Book\Controller\Form',
            'action'     => 'index',
        ),
    ),
)
```

We also need the alias Book\Controller\Form in the controller configuration. This works exactly the same as the alias we already defined for our IndexController (see Listing 6.1).

The FormController

The actual FormController has to be placed at the same level as the IndexController, and we will create it from scratch this time:

```
namespace Book\Controller;

use Zend\Mvc\Controller\AbstractActionController;

class FormController extends AbstractActionController
{
    public function indexAction()
    {

    }
}
```

This is the minimum code required to display our form, which has a static template for now. Note that the base controller lives in the Zend\Mvc\Controller namespace and is called AbstractActionController, as opposed to Zend_Controller_Action in ZF1.

Converting the Form

Now that we have all of the wiring in place and can open the exact same form in our browser, it's time to actually convert the form. So far, we have only copied the output from the ZF1 view script into the ZF2 view script, and we have gotten the same end result. But no actual ZF2 form is being used.

To change that, we first build up our form in the indexAction; however, we now use Zend\Form\Form. Its usage differs from ZF1 (see Listing 9.2). Some differences are subtle, while others are bigger. Let's look at them one by one. Please note that there is an error in Listing 9.2 that I will address later on. Therefore, do not use this as an example just yet.

Listing 9.2 Using a form in an action

```php
<?php
// @file: FormController.php
namespace Book\Controller;

use Zend\Mvc\Controller\AbstractActionController;
use Zend\Form\Form;
use Zend\Form\Element;
use Zend\View\Model\ViewModel as View;

class FormController extends AbstractActionController
{
    public function indexAction()
    {
        $form = new Form('person');
        $firstname = new Element\Text('firstname');
        $firstname->setLabel('First name');

        $lastname = new Element\Text('lastname');
        $lastname->setLabel('Last name');

        $submit = new Element\Submit('save');
        $submit->setValue('Send');
        $form
            ->add($firstname)
            ->add($lastname)
            ->add($submit);

        $view = new View();
        $view->form = $form;
        return $view;
    }
}
```

Importing the Namespaces

First of all, note our use statements near the top of the file `FormController.php`. We use `Zend\View\Model\ViewModel` as `View`, `Zend\Form\Form`, and `Zend\Form\Element`. If you are already used to namespaces, you do not need an explanation. But otherwise, you should realize that this is a way to import these namespaces so that we can use their short name or alias: `View`, `Form`, and `Element`. Any type of element we need, we can now instantiate using `new Element\{type}()`, as in `new Element\Select()`, for example.

Adding Elements

Adding these elements to the form is not done like before, by calling `addElement`, but just by calling `add` on the form object. The `add()` method is very flexible. You can use it to add elements, fieldsets, and configurations that can be parsed by the form factory. A form itself is just a special incarnation of a fieldset in ZF2, so yes, it is right that fieldsets can be nested. A collection is a repeating fieldset typically used to represent a OneToMany relationship between objects that are used as hydrators on the form (more about hydration later).

The view model is a way to pass the form to the view. Note that we could have chosen to pass a simple associative array, instead. Do not forget to *return* the view model or array from the action; otherwise, it will not reach the output.

Rendering the Elements

With the code from Listing 9.2 in place, we still do not really use our form elements. In order to use the actual elements, we need to render them in the view script. Decorators are gone. If we render an element, we can choose between several options: render the basic element using the `formInput` view helper and render other aspects, such as the label, explicitly or use the `formRow()` view helper.

This will render the element and its label in one go. Alternatively, we can write our own view helpers to render repeated sequences of HTML markup that we would otherwise consider too tedious to type.

In our example, we need explicit rendering, as we are reproducing legacy markup, generated by a default `Zend_Form` that did use decorators (see Listing 9.1). The result is in Listing 9.3. A difference that jumps to the eye immediately is that if we convert forms using this approach, we need a lot more code than we did in ZF1. What we get in return, though, is a lot of flexibility.

Listing 9.3 Replicating form markup

```php
<?php
    $firstname = $form->get('firstname');
    $lastname = $form->get('lastname');
    $submit = $form->get('save');
    $form->prepare();
    // Get the form label plugin
    $formLabel = $this->plugin('formLabel');
?>

<?= $this->form()->openTag($form) ?>
    <dl class="zend_form">
        <dt id="firstname-label">
            <label for="firstname" class="optional">
            <?= $firstname->getLabel() ?></label>
        </dt>
        <dd id="firstname-element">
            <?= $this->formInput($firstname) ?>
        </dd>
        <dt id="lastname-label">
            <label for="lastname" class="optional">
            <?= $lastname->getLabel() ?></label>
        </dt>
        <dd id="lastname-element">
            <?= $this->formInput($lastname) ?>
        </dd>
        <dt id="save-label"> </dt>
        <dd id="save-element">
            <?= $this->formInput($submit) ?>
        </dd>
    </dl>
<?= $this->form()->closeTag() ?>
```

What I did not show you here is that there are more ways to add elements and to configure forms, such as by annotating the objects that you might associate with the form as hydrators. In particular, annotations will save you a lot of typing and keep the configuration of your forms tied to your objects. It is, of course, up to you if you want that.

Comparing the Output

The output of what we have migrated so far is in Listing 9.4. What you should notice is that the form elements do not have ID attributes yet. This is different from the old output in Listing 9.1. We need to add the IDs explicitly using `setAttribute('id', 'firstname')`, for example. This was the "error" I talked about when I discussed Listing 9.2. Note that on the form itself, this works differently: the form automatically gets the name and the ID set to the same value, which is the string value the form was initialized with.

Listing 9.4 Migrated form output

```
<form action="" method="POST" name="person" id="person">
    <dl class="zend_form">
        <dt id="firstname-label">
            <label for="firstname" class="optional">First name</label>
        </dt>
        <dd id="firstname-element">
            <input type="text" name="firstname" value="" />
        </dd>
        <dt id="lastname-label">
            <label for="lastname" class="optional">Last name</label>
        </dt>
        <dd id="lastname-element">
            <input type="text" name="lastname" value="" />
        </dd>
        <dt id="save-label"> </dt>
        <dd id="save-element">
            <input type="submit" name="save" value="Send" />
        </dd>
    </dl>
</form>
```

Chapter 10

Data Validating and Filtering

Validating and filtering are often related to forms, but they can be used separately. To emphasize this and also just to keep the book well structured, I reserve this separate chapter for validation and filtering. Filtering and validating can be used against any form of data, regardless of whether forms are involved. In ZF1, validation was tied closely to forms, but you could use it separately, too, by using Zend_Filter_Input. This component has been replaced and improved by Zend\InputFilter\InputFilter. Also, the new input filter is now *the single centralized way* to filter and validate at all times.

Filtering and Validating Our Data

Suppose that we want to simply validate a 'firstname' and 'lastname', without worrying about where the data comes from. We will create an input filter, which trims whitespace from the 'firstname' and validates it against a regular expression, while it leaves the 'lastname' as is. We will do this in the FormController for convenience's sake and call the method filterAction, with a corresponding filter.phtml view and a corresponding '/Form/filter' route, that is configured as a child route of the '/Form' route:

```
'may_terminate' => true,
'child_routes' => array(
    'filter' => array(
        'type' => 'Zend\Mvc\Router\Http\Literal',
        'options' => array(
            'route' => '/filter',
            'defaults' => array(
                'action' => 'filter',
            ),
        ),
    ),
),
```

A child route is appended to the parent route. In this case, the parent route stops at the end of /Form, and that is where the child route comes in with /filter, resulting in Form/filter. If the parent changes, all child routes change. Options of the parent are inherited by the children and can be overridden. Defining child routes saves you only a little typing; it is mostly useful for restricting routes to a hierarchy.

The 'may_terminate' => true line is essential; without it, the parent route doesn't work. This is because if you use child routes, you are actually using a TreeRouteStack, and it needs to know that it is permitted and that no other segments follow after the parent part (/Form).

The filterAction is in Listing 10.1, the view script used to display the result is in Listing 10.2, and the rendered result looks like Figure 10.1. To demonstrate that it doesn't matter where the values come from, I have used a regular array filled with hardcoded data. The input filter simply doesn't care that we don't use a form.

Listing 10.1 Defining our filter action

```
/**
 * Filters and validates a dataset containing
 * a 'firstname' field
 * @return array Associative array with view data
 */
public function filterAction()
{
    $filter = new InputFilter();
    $filter->add(
        array(
            'name' => 'firstname',
            'filters' => array(
                array(
                    'name' => 'string_trim',
                ),
            ),
            'validators' => array(
                array(
                    'name' => 'regex',
                    'options' => array(
                        'pattern' => "/^[a-z]*$/i",
                    )
                ),
            ),
        )
    );
    $filter->add(array('name' => 'lastname'));

    $data = array(
        'firstname' => ' James (007) ',
        'lastname'  => 'Bond',
    );

    $filter->setData($data);

    $valid = $filter->isValid();

    // use the filtered values as view data
    $view = $filter->getValues();

    // add some information
    $view['valid'] = $valid;
    $view['messages'] = $filter->getMessages();

    // return the view data
    return $view;
}
```

Listing 10.2 Displaying filter results

```
<h1>The filtered and validated result:</h1>
<p>The quotes are there so that you can see that whitespace
is stripped off the first name</p>

<p>First name: &quot;<?php echo $firstname ?>&quot;</p>
<p>Last name: &quot;<?php echo $this->escapeHtml($lastname)?>
  &quot;</p>

<h2>
    <?php if ($valid === true) : ?>
        The data is valid.
    <?php else: ?>
        INVALID data detected!
    <?php endif ?>
</h2>
<?php if (isset($messages)) : ?>
    <?php foreach ($messages as $message) : ?>
        <p>
            <?php var_dump($message) ?>
        </p>
    <?php endforeach ?>
<?php endif ?>
```

FIGURE 10.1

The filtered and validated result:

The quotes are there so that you can see that whitespace is stripped off the first name

First name: "James (007)"

Last name: "Bond".

INVALID data detected!

array(1) { ["regexNotMatch"]=>string(54) "The input does not match against pattern '/^[a-z]*$/i'" }

However, if we pass the input filter and the data to a form, we can validate the form. In addition, when we pass an object to the form, we can have its properties populated by the form data. This process is called *hydration*. Several hydrator types are available, and you can even create your own. The simplest one just populates properties directly.

When migrating, you should be aware of the new capabilities of forms, which allows you to take full advantage of them. Having played with those will help you identify areas where they will be beneficial.

Putting Things Together

Read on to find out how an input filter and a form work together. Once you learn, you will be able to make a comparison with validation done back in ZF1, where we used to add validators to individual form elements. The following examples should give you an idea of how things have shifted and how you would best transpose your old validations to their ZF2 counterparts.

Automatic Validation

ZF2 comes with the `InputFilterAwareInterface`, which is powerful if you implement it. It basically means that you can give any object an input filter and methods to retrieve and set it and other objects can reliably use it to validate the object. That means that if we make a `PersonEntity` object `InputFilterAware`, the form will automatically use its filter to validate it.

In order to demonstrate processing and validating both the form and a person entity, I will first create a person entity. It will be called `Book\Entity\PersonEntity` (Listing 10.3 - next page).

Listing 10.3 Person Entity

```php
<?php
/**
 * ZF 1 -> ZF 2 migration
 *
 * Basic object with a very simple representation of a person
 *
 * @author Bart McLeod (mcleod@spaceweb.nl)
 */

namespace Book\Entity;

use Zend\InputFilter\InputFilterAwareInterface;
use Zend\InputFilter\InputFilterInterface;
use Book\Filter\PersonFilter;

class PersonEntity implements InputFilterAwareInterface
{
    protected $inputFilter;
    public $firstname;
    public $lastname;

    /**
     * Set input filter
     *
     * @param  InputFilterInterface $inputFilter
     * @return InputFilterAwareInterface
     */
    public function setInputFilter(
        InputFilterInterface $inputFilter)
    {
        $this->inputFilter = $inputFilter;
    }

    /**
     * Retrieve input filter
     *
     * @return InputFilterInterface
     */
    public function getInputFilter()
    {
        if (is_null($this->inputFilter)) {
            $this->inputFilter = new PersonFilter();
        }

        return $this->inputFilter;
    }
}
```

To be able to reuse the corresponding input filter, I will also create a
Book\Filter\PersonFilter (Listing 10.4).

Listing 10.4 Person Input Filter

```php
<?php
/**
 * ZF 1 -> ZF 2 migration
 *
 * Example of a custom input filter
 *
 * @author Bart McLeod (mcleod@spaceweb.nl)
 */

namespace Book\Filter;

use Zend\InputFilter\InputFilter;

class PersonFilter extends InputFilter
{
    public function __construct()
    {
        $this->add(
            array(
                'name' => 'firstname',
                'filters' => array(
                    array(
                        'name' => 'string_trim',
                    ),
                ),
                'validators' => array(
                    array(
                        'name' => 'regex',
                        'options' => array(
                            'pattern' => "/^[a-z]*$/i",
                        )
                    ),
                ),
            )
        );
        $this->add(array('name' => 'lastname'));
    }
}
```

Lastly, we will also need a Book\Form\PersonForm (Listing 10.5). Note that I repeat the
type in the name of the object, naming the form PersonForm, instead of just Person.
This is a convention that I copied from what I see in ZF2 code and code examples, but
it is not always my personal preference. Sometimes, I prefer to use short names like
Book\Entity\Person.

Listing 10.5 Person Form

```php
<?php
/**
 * ZF 1 -> ZF 2 migration
 *
 * Example of a custom form
 *
 * @author Bart McLeod (mcleod@spaceweb.nl)
 */

namespace Book\Form;

use Zend\Form\Form;
use Zend\Form\Element;

class PersonForm extends Form
{
    public function __construct($name = null,
                                $options = array())
    {
        parent::__construct($name, $options);
        $this->setupElements();
    }

    protected function setupElements()
    {
        $firstname = new Element\Text('firstname');
        $firstname
            ->setLabel('First name')
            ->setAttribute('id', 'firstname');

        $lastname = new Element\Text('lastname');
        $lastname
            ->setLabel('Last name')
            ->setAttribute('id', 'lastname');

        $submit = new Element\Submit('save');
        $submit
            ->setAttribute('id', 'save')
            ->setValue('Send');
        $this
            ->add($firstname)
            ->add($lastname)
            ->add($submit);
    }
}
```

The advanced usage examples go into another controller, the ImprovedFormController (Listing 10.6). The routes to it will begin with /Form2.

Listing 10.6 Improved Form Controller

```php
<?php
namespace Book\Controller;

use Book\Entity\PersonEntity;
use Book\Filter\PersonFilter;
use Zend\Mvc\Controller\AbstractActionController;
use Book\Form\PersonForm as Form;
use Zend\Form\Element;
use Zend\InputFilter\InputFilter;
use Zend\Stdlib\Hydrator\ObjectProperty;

class ImprovedFormController
    extends AbstractActionController
{
    /**
     * Displays the custom person form
     *
     * @return array|\Zend\View\Model\ViewModel
     */
    public function indexAction()
    {
        $form = new Form('person');
        $form->setAttribute(
            'action',
            $this->url()->fromRoute('form2/process')
        );
        return array('form' => $form);
    }

    public function processAction()
    {
        $form = new Form('person');
        $post = $this->params()->fromPost();
        $person = new PersonEntity();
        $form->setObject($person);
        $form->setHydrator(new ObjectProperty());
        $form->setData($post);

        $valid = $form->isValid() ? 'valid' : 'INVALID';
        return array(
            'valid'  => $valid
                'person' => $person,
            );
    }
}
```

Object Hydration

As you can see, the actions in this controller are much simpler than those of the FormController because the logic is now encapsulated in custom classes. There is also some added value: the form almost automatically populates a PersonEntity in its processAction. The result of the processAction is displayed by process.phtml:

```
<h1>Result</h1>
<p>
    The form is <?php echo $valid ?>
</p>
<h2>Check if the object is hydrated:</h2>
<p>
    <?php var_dump($person) ?>
</p>
```

And the output HTML source:

```
<div id="main">
    <h1>Result</h1>
<p>
    The form is valid
</p>
<h2>Check if the object is hydrated:</h2>
<p>
<!-- below is a simplified entity, before it
    was InputFilterAware -->
object(Book\Entity\PersonEntity)#271 (3) {
  ["firstname"]=&gt;
  string(4) "Bart"
  ["lastname"]=&gt;
  string(6) "McLeod"
  ["save"]=&gt;
  string(4) "Send"
}
</p></div>
```

Note that the var_dump in the above example uses a PersonEntity that is not yet InputFilterAware.

Adding a Validation Group

The scary bit is that the resulting $person object now also holds a save property with a value of Send, which is obviously not our intention. This is because the form adds every element it contains to the input filter, and I used an ObjectProperty hydrator. What you see here is the name and the value of the submit button hydrating the PersonEntity.

Nothing prevents PHP from adding the property to the PersonEntity object, even if that property is not defined. We can solve this by adding a validation group to the PersonForm. A validation group solves the problem because it specifies which inputs are allowed. The updated PersonForm is in Listing 10.7.

Listing 10.7 Form with Validation Group

```php
<?php
/**
 * ZF 1 -> ZF 2 migration
 *
 * Example of a custom form
 *
 * @author Bart McLeod (mcleod@spaceweb.nl)
 */

namespace Book\Form;

use Zend\Form\Form;
use Zend\Form\Element;

class PersonForm extends Form
{
    public function __construct($name = null,
                                $options = array())
    {
        parent::__construct($name, $options);
        $this->setupElements();
    }

    protected function setupElements()
    {
        $firstname = new Element\Text('firstname');
        $firstname
            ->setLabel('First name')
            ->setAttribute('id', 'firstname');

        $lastname = new Element\Text('lastname');
        $lastname
            ->setLabel('Last name')
            ->setAttribute('id', 'lastname');

        $submit = new Element\Submit('save');
        $submit
            ->setAttribute('id', 'save')
            ->setValue('Send');
```

Continued next page

```
        $this
            ->add($firstname)
            ->add($lastname)
            ->add($submit);


        $this->setValidationGroup(
            array(
                'firstname',
                'lastname',
            )
        );
    }
}
```

The following code was added:

```
// inside Book\Form\PersonForm::setupElements()
$this->setValidationGroup(
    array(
        'firstname',
        'lastname',
    )
);
```

Other Hydrators

To prevent malicious users from creating any property they like on your objects, you can use a hydrator that uses setter methods that you have explicitly defined: Zend\Stdlib\Hydrator\ClassMethods or Zend\Stdlib\Hydrator\ArraySerializable. The ClassMethods hydrator uses getter and setter methods that you have defined on your object, while the ArraySerializable hydrator can handle objects that implement the ArraySerializable interface.

Chapter 11

The Database

While this chapter is about *the* Database, I obviously do not believe there is *only one* database. Talking databases in modern software development is risky because you have no idea what your audience will think of when hearing the D-word. Some people may think SQLite, while others may think NoSql or Big Data. Many of us will be familiar with using MySQL as a database backend, and I am no exception.

Your existing ZF1 application might be using a database right now. It is likely that your ZF1 code interacts with it one way or the other. There are, in fact, so many different ways you might have implemented your business models (the part of your software that interacts with the data) that it is hard to tell which migration strategy would be best for you. If you are the type of person who wants to continuously improve on things (which is probably why you are reading this guide), then you will find ways to improve your business models when you look at the completely rewritten Zend\Db component or Doctrine 2 integration.

While I am relatively unfamiliar with Doctrine, I know a little about Zend_Db, and I am also using the new Zend\Db component from ZF2 in my everyday work. While Doctrine offers a complete object relation model (ORM) once configured, Zend\Db is more about the objects themselves and the interaction with the database and, if you must, relationships. Don't let me keep you from using Doctrine, though. But in this guide, I will talk about Zend\Db because it is native to ZF2, not because I think Doctrine is bad.

As a side note, it may be of importance to realize that the migration of your MVC application and database models do not necessarily happen at the same time. The migration project would grow too big if it was. You could, instead, use the old version of one next to the new version of the other as a more efficient strategy.

The only tight integration point of the database layer and the MVC is pagination. But you might be able to write a pagination adapter to overcome that. In general, if a component is interwoven with the MVC, it has to be migrated at the same time with Zend_Db only if you use paginators from ZF, as there is a coupling between the two. By exchanging the paginator adapter for a custom-built one, you can bridge that gap.

Your usage of Zend\Db may vary from plain and simple querying using the Zend\Db\Adapter\Adapter to using AbstractTableGateway or TableGateway and RowGateway, HydratingResultSet, Sql, and Expression objects.

The Model and Code Generation

Today, going loosely coupled is the mantra. To ensure maximum reuse of components for a database, you might end up with six classes per entity (more about those six classes later). If you have a database that describes two hundred different entities, that would mean you'd end up with twelve hundred classes to maintain.

Even with only twenty tables, manually maintaining one hundred and twenty classes is not a good idea. This is where code generation comes into play. Once you have a good picture of what your model classes should look like—because you tested a few of them— you can generate the rest. My approach has been to write view scripts (ZF templates) for PHP code and render those to PHP files using Zend_View.

This will work equally well using Zend\View\View. To add to the fun, we have Zend\Db\MetaData, which provides information about your database and will prove useful when generating model classes. There is a component for, among other things, code generation, called Zend\Code. By looking at the code or the API documentation, you should be able figure out how it could help in generating model classes.

When generating code, you can use Symfony as an example. For every class, you create a base class and a custom class that inherits from it. The base class holds all of the generated logic, which can be overridden in the custom class. The custom class, which is initially empty, is used in the code of your application (the code you write).

Each time your database changes, the base classes are regenerated, but the custom classes are left untouched. This way, your customizations will survive regeneration. For each model class that you generate, there is also a base class, so with twenty tables in your database, you are expected to have two hundred and forty classes, which you only customize when necessary.

Zend\Db

The six classes commonly in use when building your business model are the following:

- An object (#1) that talks to the database to read one or more records,
- An object (#2) that maps the fields from the record to an entity object (#3), and
- A service object (#4) that can get you one or many entities using method names that relate to the business logic.
- In addition, you will have an input filter (#5) and a form (#6).

Now, how does this translate to Zend\Db? Programmatically built queries abstract you away from the database system. If you use those in your objects that fulfil role 1 (talking to the database), you will be able to reuse these objects when you switch from one database system to another. I must admit, I haven't seen this in real life. When a database system was swapped for another, this was part of a larger project where the codebase, as a whole, was also replaced.

A more realistic scenario for using different database systems is when you write an application that others may install on top of various database systems following their personal preference or needs. Then, the underlying database system is outside of your control, but your application will still be compatible if there is a database adapter for it. All that would have to change is the configuration of the adapter.

Then what about the objects that map the results coming from the database to the entity objects? With Zend\Db, by default, you get back a ResultSet object, which contains elements of the ArrayObject class. If you use a custom result set object, you can specify (in the constructor) which class the elements returned should have. So you can specify your own entity class, which means that your result set takes care of the mapping, with the actual mapping done by a hydrator.

Now, the general purpose of a mapper is to be independent of the field names and the way they are returned from the database. What kind of hydrator and result set would we need to accomplish that independence? A HydratingResultSet can take an instance of a hydrator (in our case, ObjectProperty) and an entity (PersonEntity) and will thus deliver hydrated PersonEntity instances while you loop over it in your code.

This hydrator maps properties that match fields names. So if we want a hydrator that matches differing names, we need to do something extra. Although I am tempted to show you some examples right now, we should first take one step back and look at some simple and practical examples.

Zend\Db Examples

Let's consider the PersonEntity from the forms chapter. How would we persist it to a database using Zend\Db? The easiest way is to use a concrete TableGateway. I risk repeating the manual here, but I think that you should be able to follow along with this, so I'll hazard that. A concrete TableGateway should be instantiated with a table name and a database adapter. After that, it is ready to start interacting with that table. If MySQL is my example database system and my database is named book, then I need a person table in the book database:

```
CREATE TABLE `person` (
 `id` int(11) unsigned NOT NULL AUTO_INCREMENT,
 `firstname` varchar(100) NOT NULL,
 `lastname` varchar(100) NOT NULL,
 PRIMARY KEY (`id`)
) ENGINE=InnoDB DEFAULT CHARSET=utf8
```

The ImprovedFormController is now extended with two actions, a newAction and a saveAction. The newAction only serves to give the form a different action attribute, so it now posts to the saveAction. A database adapter is already configured for the application under the key Zend\Db\Adapter\Adapter. In order to add flexibility, the save action gets it using the alias Book\Db, which is defined in Book\Module::getServiceConfig() under the aliases key. I have changed the form2 route to a segment route that matches any action defined in the ImprovedFormController:

```
'form2' => array(
    'type' => 'Zend\Mvc\Router\Http\Segment',
    'options' => array(
        'route'    => '/Form2[/:action]',
        'defaults' => array(
            'controller' => 'Book\Controller\Form2',
            'action'     => 'index',
        ),
    ),
),
```

The 'new' action reuses the template from the 'index' action so that it displays the form. When the form is submitted, it posts to the 'save' action, which populates the PersonEntity in the same way as in the 'process' action we used for the forms example. Next it tries to save the person to the database:

```
if ($form->isValid()) {
    $adapter = $this->getServiceLocator()->get('Book\Db');
    $personTable = new TableGateway('person', $adapter);
    $personData = $person->getInputFilter()->getValues();
    $result = $personTable->insert($personData);
} else {
    $result = $form->getMessages();
}
```

The result is displayed in the save.phtml template:

```
<h1>The result of saving the person</h1>
<?php echo var_dump($result) ?>
```

If invalid input is provided, the error messages are dumped to the output; otherwise, the number of affected rows (1) is displayed. If you wanted to know the ID of the person in the database, you'd call $personTable->getLastInsertValue().

Of course, you might want to check if the person entity already exists in the database before trying to insert it, so you can use the form for editing existing person entities. This is the normal, tedious process when dealing with database records. It means that the person entity will need to be extended with an ID property; otherwise, we can't identify it. The same is true for the input filter and the form.

A Custom Table Object

Instead of using a concrete TableGateway object, you might want to use a custom table object. To make that easy, there is the AbstractTableGateway to extend from. In its most basic implementation, we need to set the $table property to person and add a constructor, which sets the adapter (see Listing 11.1).

Listing 11.1 PersonTable Class

```php
<?php
namespace Book\Table;

use Zend\Db\TableGateway\AbstractTableGateway;

class PersonTable extends AbstractTableGateway
{
    protected $table = 'person';

    public function __construct($adapter)
    {
        $this->adapter = $adapter;
    }
}
```

For demonstration purposes, I will create a PersonController and a segment route, which allows us to call any action on the PersonController at the URL /person[/:action]. The default index action will display our custom PersonForm again, while we reuse the template. The save action looks exactly like the one in the ImprovedFormController, except it uses our new PersonTable class to save the person entity. In this case, I have duplicated the template save.phtml into the directory view/book/person, so this action uses its own.

A RowGateway Saves Itself

When querying the table object in order to retrieve person entities, you get back a ResultSet with ArrayObject's by default. By specifying a RowGatewayFeature, you can get back RowGateway objects, which are able to save or delete themselves. In other words, if you teach your table object about the primary key of the entities it handles, it will return result sets populated with row gateway objects which know where they live in the database.

FIGURE 11.1

To demonstrate this, we need an action on our controller: the detailsAction. It will simply display the firstname and lastname of the person and the object's classname (Figure 11.1).

Details

First name: Bart

Last name: McLeod

Class name ArrayObject.

As you can see, the class name of the object returned from the details action is ArrayObject. This is the code of the details action:

```
$adapter = $this->getServiceLocator()->get('Book\Db');
$personTable = new PersonTable($adapter);
$result = $personTable->select(array('id' => 1));
return array('person' => $result->current());
```

To add the capability to retrieve RowGateway objects from our table object, we have to add a RowGatewayFeature. To demonstrate this, I use a new person table object named PersonRowTable (see Listing 11.2), and I change the save action to use this class, instead.

Listing 11.2 PersonRowTable Class

```php
<?php
namespace Book\Table;

use Zend\Db\TableGateway\AbstractTableGateway;
use Zend\Db\TableGateway\Feature\FeatureSet;
use Zend\Db\TableGateway\Feature\RowGatewayFeature;

class PersonRowTable extends AbstractTableGateway
{
    protected $table = 'person';

    public function __construct($adapter)
    {
        $this->adapter = $adapter;
        $this->featureSet = new FeatureSet();
        $this->getFeatureSet()->addFeature(
            new RowGatewayFeature('id')
        );
    }
}
```

Now the output of the details action (Figure 11.2) shows that the array returned when querying through the table object gets us Zend\Db\RowGateway\RowGateway objects, which allow us to save the object back to the database.

FIGURE 11.2

Details

First name: Bart

Last name: McLeod

Class name Zend\Db\RowGateway\RowGateway.

This is only useful if you want to change the properties of the object from within your code after you retrieved it from the database. It does nothing magical to form input processing. If you get input from the form and want to know whether the record exists, you'll still have to check to make sure that the 'id' property is not empty.

Back to Hydrating

When we discussed the six different classes you might use per table to obtain a loosely coupled business model, I pointed at the possibility of using a hydrator as a mapper. If your field names match the names of your object properties, you may use a simple hydrator that ships with the Zend\StdLib in ZF2. It is used in conjunction with a HydratingResultset, which you may specify inside the constructor of your custom table object. Alternatively, you could use setter injection on the same object by defining a setter method for the $resultSetPrototype property.

For our examples, I will use the constructor and not even inject it. Instead, I'll set it directly in the constructor of a new type of table object, the PersonHydratorTable. This cannot be used together with the RowGatewayFeature. The latter expects a regular result set to be returned from the table object, not a HydratingResultSet.

```
class PersonHydratorTable extends AbstractTableGateway
{
    protected $table = 'person';

    public function __construct($adapter)
    {
        $this->adapter = $adapter;
        $this->resultSetPrototype =
            new HydratingResultSet(
                new ObjectProperty(), new PersonEntity()
            );
    }
}
```

In the hydrate action of the personController, you will see the following code, which cause the fields of the form to be populated with the values of the PersonEntity object:

```
$id = (int) $this->getEvent()->getRouteMatch()->getParam('id');
$adapter = $this->getServiceLocator()->get('Book\Db');
$personTable = new PersonHydratorTable($adapter);
$result = $personTable->select(array('id' => $id));
$person = $result->current();
$form->setHydrator(new ObjectProperty());
$form->bind($person);
```

Two things are essential in the previous code snippet. First of all, we use a PersonHydratorTable instance, which uses a HydratingResultSet internally. As a result, it returns a set of populated PersonEntity objects. In this case, because we use a single id in our query, it contains a single entity. Secondly, we set a simple ObjectProperty hydrator on the form and call its bind method while passing it the populated entity. Now the form will extract the values from the object by means of the hydrator, and thus, the result of the hydrate action will be a form with pre-filled values.

In real-life code, if you wanted to handle fifty different entities, you would probably configure your controllers with pre-configured table objects (through setter injection), and you would probably introduce either a base controller or, possibly better, an Id plugin that would deliver the ID from the parameters. Or you might have just a single controller for handling entities, which figures out which entity it should handle by inspecting the route match. That is all up to you; I only hope to inspire by showing you some of the great possibilities available with Zend\Db.

Service Objects

We have looked at almost every object that a loosely coupled model should encompass. We have seen the table object, which talks to the database. We have seen the entity object and how we can use an out-of-the-box hydrator to act as a very simple mapper. We have seen the form and the input filter. We haven't yet seen the service object, which can deliver one or more entities in a way that relates to your business domain. But you are good at that already, as it is your business domain.

Remember to give it a datasource. In our example, the datasource would be our table object. By using Zend\Db\Sql either directly or by calling $this->getSql() inside the table object, we can programmatically build queries. This gives you great power, especially if you need to change the query dynamically—for example, to set an offset and a limit.

By setting the datasource on the service object, the service object will not need to do much more than some post-processing on the data retrieved and map to methods on the datasource. The advantage is that if your datasource changes, ideally, you only have to write new datasource classes and configure your service objects with those.

The code consuming the services should be able to stay the same. Of course, this is only necessary if your datasource changes considerably—for example, from a database to a web service. When only the database system changes, all you should need to do is modify the adapter configuration.

We haven't looked at complex mappers, but I have no doubt that you will be able to write your own hydrator once you get the basic concept.

Chapter 12

Development Practices

Configuring Different Environments

In ZF1, we were used to have different sections in `application.ini`, like Production, Testing, and Development, and often a few personal developer sections, like `'dev_bart'`. By setting an environment variable, you could easily distinguish between environments and, for example, load different database credentials. In ZF2, this is solved in a different manner.

Let's take database configuration: Imagine you built a module that uses a MySQL database. You might have configured the database adapter with the key `db_adapter_book` inside your module configuration.

Note: If you want to make your module reusable, you should consider *not* configuring your database adapter within your module, but instead let the users of your module decide how they configure the database and only provide them with guidance. This is how ZfcUser configuration works.

However, you may not want to be bothered with making your module reusable at all. You might just want to configure your database adapter. Now you might or might not be bothered by security issues, *but you should be.* Therefore, it is not a good idea to store valid credentials inside your module configuration, for those will end up in your versioning system, and that's not where you want them from a security perspective. You still need a place to store an example configuration, which is tied to your module.

For the example configuration, the module is not a bad place at all. Once you have that, you will need a place to override it per environment.

Enter local.php and global.php

In your ZendSkeletonApplication you will find a directory called config/autoload. In there, you have a local.php and a global.php file. These are used to override module-specific settings for your environment. In global.php, you will store settings every module might need, whereas in local.php, you can override those, as well as settings from any module configuration. In addition, any file *ending* with local.php or global.php can be used in this way.

In our case, we can create book.local.php to override the database adapter configuration from the book module. Files ending with local.php will not be committed to git because of the default .gitignore file, thus keeping you from inadvertently adding those database credentials to version control. An example adapter configuration could look like this:

```
return array(
    'service_manager' => array(
        'factories' => array(
            'db_adapter_book' => function ($sm) {
                return new Zend\Db\Adapter\Adapter(array(
                    'driver'    => 'pdo_mysql',
                    'database'  => 'book',
                    'username'  => 'foouser',
                    'password'  => 'secret',
                    'hostname'  => 'localhost',
                ));
            },
        ),
    ),
);
```

You may override this for your local development in book.local.php.

Inheritance of Configuration

If we take the above code snippet, we should spot that there is a lot of duplication if we override this configuration. This is simply because most of it won't change. For example, you might have three environments where only the password changes. We can solve this by configuring the parameters for the database adapter and overriding only the password.

```php
// in local.php
return array(
    'view_manager' => array(
        'display_exceptions'       => true,
        'display_not_found_reason' => true,
    ),
    'db_password' => 'root',
);
```

And in the database adapter configuration of the module:

```php
'Zend\Db\Adapter\Adapter' => function ($sm) {
    $config = $sm->get('Config');
    return new Adapter(array(
        'driver'    => 'pdo_mysql',
        'database'  => 'book',
        'username'  => 'root',
        'password'  => $config['db_password'],
        'hostname'  => 'localhost',
    ));
},
```

It looks as if we now have a dependency on the db_adapter_book key or the Zend\Db\Adapter\Adapter key, but aliases come to the rescue. Say you want to use the Book module but already have a database adapter configured (db_foo), and you have installed all of the tables of the Book module in the same database that db_foo connects to.

In such a case, you would want to reuse the db_foo connection for the Book module. There are at least two ways in which this can be accomplished.

Re-using a Database Adapter

The first way is to simply modify the configuration for db_adapter_book in book.global.php so that it gets the db adapter db_foo:

```
return array(
    'service_manager' => array(
        'factories' => array(
            'db_adapter_book' => function ($sm) {
                return $sm->get('db_foo'),
            },
        ),
    ),
);
```

It is much simpler to just configure an alias, instead:

```
return array(
    'service_manager' => array(
        'aliases' => array(
            'db_adapter_book' => 'db_foo',
        ),
    ),
);
```

Note that when overriding the configuration for the database adapter in book.global.php, to reuse an existing adapter, you are telling the application to do this in every environment. In this case, you should *not* also override the database adapter configuration in book.local.php, unless you specifically want to use yet another adapter for that specific environment.

Configuring a Key

ZfcUser takes a slightly different approach. It lets you *configure* which configuration key you use for the database adapter that connects to the database where you installed the ZfcUser tables. If you configured it, it will use that as an alias, as in the above example; otherwise, it will use the key Zend\Db\Adapter\Adapter, assuming that you have configured it that way.

Third-party Modules

User management is probably one of the most common areas where we all write boilerplate code, instead of focusing on what matters in our business domain. This is a typical case where reusing modules that others have written can come to the rescue.

Zend Framework Commons is a group of developers who aim to create reusable modules. One of those modules is ZfcUser[1]. When doing a migration, you should keep an eye on already-existing modules. Wouldn't it be nice if you could eliminate a lot of your own code and replace it with code that is maintained and tested by others?

Integrating ZfcUser

ZfcUser depends on ZfcBase. In order to use it, you can either install it with composer (and have the dependency installed automatically) or clone both repositories into vendor, as I have done:

```
sudo git clone https://github.com/ZF-Commons/ZfcUser.git
sudo git clone https://github.com/ZF-Commons/ZfcBase.git
```

Both modules need to be enabled in the config/application.config.php configuration file. You also need to install a database table. The table structure is in the files that come with the ZfcUser module in the ZfcUser/data directory. You can also use your own database table and configure ZfcUser with the columns specific to your situation.

For my example Book module, I have simply created a book database schema in MySQL and loaded the ZfcUser/data/schema.mysql.sql file into that as follows:

```
mysql -uroot -proot book < schema.mysql.sql
```

With the user table in place and the module enabled, all that needs to be done is to copy ZfcUser/config/zfcuser.global.php.dist to config/autoload/zfcuser.global.php. Next, configure a key for the database adapter, or you may configure the database adapter if you do not already have one configured. In the case of the Book module, a database adapter is configured for the book database as a service factory in Module::getServiceConfig():

```
// in array return from Module::getServiceConfig()
// under the key 'factories'
'Zend\Db\Adapter\Adapter' => function ($sm) {
    return new Adapter(array(
            'driver'    => 'pdo_mysql',
            'database'  => 'book',
            'username'  => 'root',
            'password'  => 'root',
            'hostname'  => 'localhost',
    ));
},
```

By configuring it with the key Zend\Db\Adapter\Adapter, it is immediately usable for ZfcUser. ZfcUser can easily be configured with a different key if it suits you better. Once the two modules are enabled, you can use all of the ready-made features of ZfcUser: you can login at http://book/user

[1]   ZfcUser Documentation *https://github.com/ZF-Commons/ZfcUser/wiki/*

To get the authentication from the `ServiceManager`:

```
$auth = $sm->get('zfcuser_auth_service');
```

Composer Installations

Many developers see the benefits of a dependency manager when doing installations. Composer is a dependency manager for PHP[2]. This means that if, for example, you download the `ZendSkeletonApplication` and run `php composer.phar install` from within it, it will download and install the `ZF2` library for you. Equally, if you use it to install `ZfcUser`, it will install `ZfcBase`, as well, because `ZfcUser` depends on it. A composer installation is configured using a `composer.json` file. In the json file, you specify which version of the package you want. After that, you run:

```
php composer.phar install
```

That's all there is to it. If you run the composer a second time, you need to run `update`, instead of `install`, because the composer locks the initial installation using a `composer.lock` file.

If the composer issues a warning that it is more than 30 days old, you should definitely follow its advice and run `php composer.phar self-update` first to avoid problems during subsequent installations.

The composer file in a standard `ZendSkeletonApplication` looks like this:

```
{
    "name": "zendframework/skeleton-application",
    "description": "Skeleton Application for ZF2",
    "license": "BSD-3-Clause",
    "keywords": [
        "framework",
        "zf2"
    ],
    "homepage": "http://framework.zend.com/",
    "require": {
        "php": ">=5.3.3",
        "zendframework/zendframework": ">2.2.0rc1"
    }
}
```

[2]   http://getcomposer.org/

If we want to add ZfcUser, we should add this to the require section of the composer configuration.

```
"require": {
    "php": ">=5.3.3",
    "zendframework/zendframework": ">2.2.0rc1",
    "zf-commons/zfc-user": "dev-master"
}
```

Or use the following command to add it automatically:

```
composer require zf-commons/zfc-user:dev-master
```

www.ingramcontent.com/pod-product-compliance
Lightning Source LLC
Chambersburg PA
CBHW080426220326
41519CB00071BA/7253